Dragon Slayers

DR. TANIA WISEMAN

ISBN 978-1-0980-4863-1 (paperback)
ISBN 978-1-0980-4864-8 (digital)

Copyright © 2020 by Dr. Tania Wiseman

All rights reserved. No part of this publication may be reproduced, distributed, or transmitted in any form or by any means, including photocopying, recording, or other electronic or mechanical methods without the prior written permission of the publisher. For permission requests, solicit the publisher via the address below.

Christian Faith Publishing, Inc.
832 Park Avenue
Meadville, PA 16335
www.christianfaithpublishing.com

All scripture quotations used are taken from the King James Version (public domain)

Printed in the United States of America

The Rose

He is the Rose of Sharon
And the morning star that shines deep within
Conquering perils of life
Matures my gift of grace from sin.
Majestic spells the flavor
That fill the earth below,
But ere I search, higher does my spirit soar
To a plane far, far above where reach of
moth and rust dare not touch.
Streets of gold
Nor gates of pearl
Doth hold a candle to
His beauty dwelling there.
A thousand sunsets I am told
My eyes shall grace when I behold
The morning star, the rose.

CONTENTS

Introduction..7
Chapter 1: Listen Up 9
Chapter 2: Know the Enemy 23
Chapter 3: Gotta Get Dressed..35
Chapter 4: True Weapons 46
Chapter 5: Prepare for War 59
Chapter 6: Use of the Unexpected...69
Chapter 7: Lots of Prayers 79
Chapter 8: Secret Weapon..90
Chapter 9: What Satan Saw 99
Chapter 10: Power in Praise 108
Chapter 11: Receive Him..114

INTRODUCTION

When I was a child, my grandfather Claude Polley Sr. would tell me stories of Bible heroes. He called them *dragon slayers*. I would be a warrior, a dragon slayer, one day. That was what he would always say.

This book is dedicated to all the dragon slayers, warriors. Its purpose is to help you to understand who you are in Christ and to believe what the Word says about you. Walk hand in hand with our beloved Jesus. You are a dragon slayer. Now get dressed and get out there. Dragons are roaming loose.

(Please note that King James Bible were used for all scriptures. *Roget's 21st Century Thesaurus*, New *Webster's Dictionary*, and *Roget's Thesaurus* were used as well.)

Chapter 1

Listen Up

Long ago when the enemies of the children of Israel and of God went to war, they fought until every one of the enemy tribe was completely wiped out. Sometimes even the horses and goats were killed off. The children of God, his chosen people, would seek him out to know how to win, what to do, and where to fight.

In Numbers is the story of Caleb and the promised land. While the Israelites were camped in the wilderness after leaving Egypt, Moses sent twelve men out, one from each of the tribes, to look over the promised land and assess the strength of its inhabitants. Representing the tribe of Judah was Caleb, and representing the tribe of Ephraim was Joshua. Ten spies were intimidated by the inhabitants of Canaan, returning with evil reports of the land. But Caleb, being bold in the Lord, urged the Israelites to invade and occupy the promised land. Joshua agreed with him that they could win the battle.

Losing faith that the Lord would protect them, the children murmured against Moses and Aaron and wanted to choose a leader and return to Egypt. When Caleb and Joshua urged them to maintain their faith in the Lord's protection and move on into Canaan, they were pelted with stones.

God punished the children by making them remain in the wilderness for decades longer until the disobedient generation, except only Caleb and Joshua, died out.

After the years of the desert wandering were over and Canaan was being parceled out among the Israelite tribes, Caleb was allotted land and villages in the vicinity of Hebron. At the age of eighty-five, Caleb claimed to be as strong as he had been a generation earlier when he first traveled through Canaan as a spy and proved his prowess by driving out the inhabitants, and as the Lord instructed, the promised land was taken in battle.

Caleb and Joshua kept their faith in God for protection and safety and did not doubt the Lord's instructions to take the land. They did not see anything but winning, overcoming, and trusting the Lord. They kept focused on God.

A mighty warrior of God was David. His story is in 1 Samuel. The armies of the Philistines and Israelites confronted one another from the opposite sides of the valley of Elah, west of Bethlehem. Every day Goliath, the Philistines' champion, stepped out into the valley and insulted the Israelites. He would challenge any warrior to single combat with national victory and servitude hanging in the balance.

Goliath stood nearly ten feet tall and sheathed in all the finest armor and weaponry of his time. He couldn't get even Saul, a mighty warrior and then king, to meet his challenges.

When David arrived at the front lines, he heard Goliath of Gath's challenge, and David boldly expressed contempt for such a man who "would defy the armies of the living God" (1 Sam. 17:26). Before Saul, David volunteered to fight Goliath. Saul listened to David's boast of killing lions and bears and of his trust in God and finally let David go meet the great giant. Offering his own armor, Saul watched as David went out with only a sling and five smooth stones.

> David looked at Goliath and said: Thou comest to me with a sword, and with a spear, and with a shield; but I come to thee in the name of

the Lord of hosts, the God of the armies of Israel, whom thou hast defied.

This day will the Lord deliver thee into mine hand; and I will smite thee, and take thine head from thee; and I will give the carcases of the host of the Philistines this day unto the fowls of the air, and to the wild beasts of the earth; that all the earth may know that there is a God in Israel. (1 Sam. 17:45-46)

David killed Goliath and beheaded him with his own sword. David never let the fear seize him or lose faith in God. He never doubted but believed God was bigger and had the victory.

Samson's great battles with the Philistines started almost immediately after his wedding. His story is in Judges. This being more of a personal battle, God still was able to use him to move Israel in the direction it needed to go. King David finished the job; he crushed the Philistines and ended their dominance in the region, but let's go back to Samson.

Though Samson had incredible strength of body, he had a weakness toward immoral women, a temper that forced him to kill thirty innocent bystanders which started the conflict that led him to kill many. A sorry life you may say, but he was still used by God to get Israel going in the right direction.

"And Samson called unto the Lord, and said, O Lord God, remember me, I pray thee, only this once, O God, that I may be at once avenged of the Philistines for my two eyes" (Judg. 16:28).

And God heard him, and he killed many, three thousand on the rooftop alone, more in death did he kill than in his life.

The Bible is full of battles, heroes, and the Lord's leading. He uses people that you would probably reject or wouldn't think worthy of the task. He still uses people today in ways that others think not worthy or smart enough for the task. To have a willing heart to be used by God is the only criteria. He will work it all out from there.

In today's hubbub of daily life, the average Christian comes home from the grind of work to face the children, the wife or husband, dinner, homework, and perhaps house chores before falling into bed. The months slipped by, and another year closed without any real hand-to-hand combat with the enemy of all Christians—the devil! Sunday sermons slipped passively by and rolled off your back. No attention was really given to circumstances along the course of the year to such things as the flu circling several times in the house or the problems your marriage suddenly developed or the teen that behaved at one time now has a behavioral problem. Symptoms of an old knee injury suddenly cropped up or troubles on the job with coworkers. All of these situations came and left in your life, and you never even so much as took a war stance, let alone declared war! And then you want to know why the devil torments you, why everything happens to you.

The enemy is playing havoc at every turn with God's children, and we are allowing him to get away with it! We have got to pay attention to his sly attacks. Our very existence depends on it. The enemy's plan is to annihilate literally every born again-human on this planet.

Christians are allowing the enemy to slip in here and there in their lives and homes. Chaos is opening up on every hand in some households. Some are just being chipped away at quietly, and no attention is being paid as the devil steals everything you have. The devil has had thousands of years to perfect his ploys on mankind, but don't despair; the answer is within our grasp—warfare!

Throughout the Bible, we see one after the other occasions and persons waging warfare against the enemies of God's people. Time after time, warfare was needed and used. Strategies, answers, and help were given from the Lord to his people. Defeat is gained by the enemy from us when we pretend things are all right or that things will work themselves out. No, real battles have to be fought to get victory. Real tactics must be used to defend your home, life, children, and circumstances. Besides, real attacks from the devil against your health, marriage, job, and mind are ongoing from him whether you're aware of it or not. Our minds are the battlefield at times, battles with good, consciousness of the sense of guilt or innocence and perception of what passes through your mind.

While one person is attacked by marital trouble, another is attacked in their mind, say, over soft pornography, or attacked from guilt for not being someone's doormat that day. There are many different attacks the enemy flings at us and lies he feeds us if we aren't on guard.

So how do we back the devil down, Tania? How do we get the victory over him in everyday living? The answers are in the Word, so let's see how to defend ourselves.

The first thing to look up is faith. As God's people, we must be filled and be strong in faith. Mark 11:24 is the heart of what is from verses 22–26, but let's cover them all.

> And Jesus answering saith unto them, Have faith in God. Which means to have faith of God. God is full of faith and we must be also.
>
> For verily I say unto you, That whosoever shall say unto this mountain, Be thou removed, and be thou cast into the sea; and shall not doubt in his heart, but shall believe that those things which he saith shall come to pass; he shall have whatsoever he saith.
>
> Therefore I say unto you, What things soever ye desire, when ye pray, believe that ye receive them, and ye shall have them.
>
> And when ye stand praying, forgive, if ye have ought against any: that your Father also which is in heaven may forgive you your trespasses.
>
> But if ye do not forgive, neither will your Father which is in heaven forgive your trespasses.

There are five steps here to be done:

1. Have the faith as God has.
2. Speak doubt not and believe what you say will come to pass.
3. Believe in advance that what you pray for, you have already received them and you shall have them.
4. Forgive others so you will be forgiven.
5. If you don't forgive others, neither will you be forgiven.

What is faith? Faith is laying ahold of the unseen realities of hope and bringing them into being a reality by acting on what God tells us in his Word.

For example, if you have a career move to make and you just received your masters in psychology and you speak in prayer that you believe the job opening you desire to God and believe you've already received it by faith, doubt not in your heart. Give any and all to the Father, and don't go back on what you're believing for. That job will come. You literally brought it from unseen to seen. Your faith got a hold of the unseen reality and brought it right into being the seen, and you worked there in that field in the job you prayed for and believed in. You worked your faith. You exercised it and did not take the lesser job the enemy sent your way. No, you stood your ground and kept believing no matter how it all looked until it became a reality. Believing and receiving is acting on the Word and causing the results to literally materialize before you.

"For we walk by faith, not by sight" (2 Cor 5:7).

You have got to get this in your spirit, man, for the first thing the old devil loves to do is shake your faith. He knows if you get this—I mean, really get it—he is defeated before he even enters the arena.

"But that no man is justified by the law in the sight of God, it is evident; for the just shall live by faith" (Gal 3:11).

This is why I say, "Get this in your spirit, man," because if you're God's, you will live by faith. It will become a lifestyle that must be mastered.

"Now the just shall live by faith: but if any man draw back, my soul shall have no pleasure in him. But we are not of them who draw back unto perdition; but of them that believe to the saving of the soul" (Heb 10:38–39).

Perdition means destruction, disruption, waste, ruin, cataclysm, subversion.

"Now faith is the substance of things hoped for, the evidence of things not seen" (Heb 11:1).

Faith is a substance. Substance is quantity, measure, strength, inner part, inward, idea, aim, design.

"But without faith it is impossible to please him; for he that cometh to God must believe that he is, and that he is a rewarder of them that diligently seek him" (Heb 11:6).

Diligence is having energy, zeal, exertion, devotion, and earnestness. The Word clearly says we are to walk and live by faith. The principles of the Word works because God does not lie. If you live and walk by faith, speak and believe what you pray for, go to him and believe he is and is a rewarder to you as you persevere and steadily go after him, and forgive others; your unseen reality will be seen realities.

Each time you flex and use your faith and exercise it, it grows, becomes stronger, has more endurance. By using your faith, you cause it to move, to be put into action, forcing it to bring forward your spoken words. Each time you flex your faith, the enemy doesn't want you to grow in faith and learn to take authority over him, and he will come at you, so be prepared. It is a much easier battle for him if he can shake your faith, put doubt in your heart, and have you get your eyes on the situation instead of on Jesus where you need to be focusing. His ploy is to keep you weak, down, discouraged, and not interested in the rules of life and war.

"Beat your plow shares into swords, and your pruning hooks into spears: let the weak say, I am strong" (Joel 3:10).

When we find ourselves weak, we are to say we are strong. Jesus is Lord over all, and in him we are made strong when we are weak. Ask him to strengthen you.

Exercise your faith and let it grow as you use faith on your daily conduct and speech. Instead of telling your teen he is no good, tell him he is a winner, a good student. Feed him constructive guidance and watch him turn around and be the faith-filled spoken words you've pronounced over him. You will be taking authority over the enemy where your child is concerned, building and flexing faith and standing your ground. Later as you need bigger and more faith in other circumstances, you'll be accustomed to speaking and believing for the faith. You can't expect to have sudden great faith if you don't exercise it daily. Start living and walking in faith daily, and you'll see what I mean.

Oh, Tania, I tried that faith stuff, and it didn't work. Quitting because you failed or forgot to use it is not going to bring the victory you need over the devil either, so dust yourself off and start again. Get so good at walking by faith that the devil gets cold shivers when you wake up in the morning.

"Through faith we understand that the worlds were framed by the word of God, so that things which are seen were not made of things which do appear" (Heb 11:3).

God spoke into being all that is. God is faith filled, and we are made in his image. We are to have faith like his.

> "And calleth those things which be not as though they were" (Rom 4:17).

Faith overcomes every circumstance. Diligently put faith in your heart, mind, and mouth. Faith comes by hearing and hearing by the word of God (Rom 10:17).

There are five steps to maintaining daily faith:

1. Seek out the Word that covers your problem and circumstance.
2. Meditate on it.
3. Tell the Lord. He wants to hear you give him the worries.
4. Speak to it and take authority over it in Jesus's name. Stand your ground.
5. Give the Lord praise and thanks for what he is doing and bringing about on your behalf.

Going to church and Bible studies is fine, and being part of fellowship is too, but there comes a time when you have to take ahold and apply the Word daily over every area of your life and know what the Word says. This is a fight for your soul. The devil is alive and hates you. He is out to destroy you at any cost and does not play fairly. The enemy is after you and what is yours and is coming after you any way he can. This is survival, yours, and the sooner you grasp this, the better chance you have. Sunday-service Christians don't have a chance in this arena of the fittest. Yes, they are saved, but that doesn't keep the devil from grabbing you and turning your life into a living hell. Leaving it to the preachers and prayer warriors only leaves you wide open for attack by the roaring lion.

Faith pleases God:

1. Walk and live by faith.
2. Speak things that are not as though they are.
3. Believe and doubt not.

4. Believe God is and diligently seek him.
5. Give him praise and thanks.

> "For we which have believed do enter into rest, as he said, as I have sworn in my wrath, if they shall enter into my rest: although the works were finished from the foundation of the world. There remaineth therefore a rest to the people of God" (Heb 4:3, 9).

Even though we are in battle, the battle is his, not ours, and we can have God's rest even in the middle of the storm.

> "Let us therefore come boldly unto the throne of grace, that we may obtain mercy, and find grace to help in time of need" (Heb 4:16).

When Satan comes knocking on the door, get before God and boldly ask for what you need. If you find you lack, get before the throne and ask. Things come up besides just in battle.

There is a rest for us to be entered into for us that believe. Rest also from work, the day of rest, the Sabbath. We have the right to go to the throne boldly.

Grace means favor, kindness, and love of God. In faith we go before God to his throne, and our faith pleases him, and we find grace in time of our need. "Let us hold fast the profession of our faith without wavering (for he is faithful that promised)" (Heb 10:23).

We are to hold on to the speaking of our faith and not waver but stay strong and firm in what we say. So many fail because they waver. I have done it too. They don't see immediate results, or the situation looks worse, and the devil scares them off from the victory and steals their possessions from them. They give up sometimes too easily. It's hard to keep hold and not quit when it doesn't look like anything is changing, but we have to remember that it takes time in some situations to call forth what is not as though it is. You have to get this want-to-win attitude way down deep in your heart and spirit.

Get it settled that you are like a pit bull and ahold of faith and not let go until what you're believing for is before you. We have all had failures, but it was us and not God that quit. Repent and pick up where you left off and reposition yourself again with a deeper understanding and commit yourself to victory no matter how long it takes.

"So then faith cometh by hearing, and hearing by the word of God" (Rom 10:17).

The Word of God is alive and is full of life to us his children. Faith comes from hearing this Word, and so faith is alive too and alive with the life of God. We have living faith in us. The devil uses no holds barred to kill and stop this faith from growing because he knows it is alive and can hurt him, stop him, and do him in. He knows that if this faith is allowed to grow and you become all in Jesus that you're supposed to be, he is defeated, lost your soul, let you get the victory, and you crushed him under your feet.

"For by grace are ye saved through faith; and not of yourselves: it is a gift of God" (Eph 2:8). Being in the Word daily is doing several things in us:

1. God speaks to us—fellowship.
2. Meditation on the Word *fills us with faith.*
3. Being faith filled *lets Jesus be head of our lives.*
4. The Word feeds *us in spirit the strength to handle the world and the devil.*
5. Faith is built *for further maturity of the inner image of who we are and what we are in Jesus.*
6. We are filled with praise *for how good God is and for how he helps us.*

Prayer does not make faith work; faith makes prayer work. "And Jesus answered him, saying, It is written, that man shall not live by bread alone, but by every word of God" (Luke 4:4).

Faith grows in us by and from the Word. "Even so faith, if it hath not works, is dead, being alone" (Jas 2:17). Faith has to have action, faith with words spoken. Believing and not doubting moves mountains and brings forth from the supernatural into the natural. Speak faith-filled words and act as if the manifestation has already taken place. Belief in the spoken words, you say, is what makes it come to pass. Have faith in your faith. Look to God and his Word. There is an answer for every situation in there. Quit looking to the world for the answers. If you've noticed, they look to us for answers because they have none that work. The world offers problems but not answers, stress and long hours but not peace and rest, unbelief but not faith-filled belief and mountain-moving action.

Stick to the Word and trust in the Lord in all things. You can't lose. Invest time into what the Word says and how to do things to get results. Be a full-time Christian, not just on Sundays and letting the pastor do it all. Realize that the enemy is real, and defeating you is only until you start flexing those faith muscles. Run fear out and replace it with faith and victory. Fear is not of God, and being his means to be like him. God is full of faith, and we must be too. Too many saints are full of fear, and defeat surrounds them. Break free, turn the tables on the enemy, and blast him with faith. Make him get up wondering what just threw him back. Be a saint to be reckoned with. We are great and mighty warriors through Jesus, not doormats for the devil and his imps!

In working and believing our faith comes patience. Waiting for your manifestation into the natural takes patience. Learning God's ways takes time and practice and patience. Building your faith stronger and stronger takes patience.

As you work on having patience, you'll find that in patience brings rest. Resting and waiting as patience is established are weapons against the devil. It allows us time to regroup, to see where we are and what to do next, to hear from God, to rest and look at things anew, to refresh the mind and body. Mature and let faith grow.

While the story of Job is of sorrow and woe, it is also of patience, waiting and resting on Job's part. In his attack from the devil, his life went from happy, full of prosperity and health, to tragedy. In his tragedy, he hung on as his wife told him to just curse God and be done with it. His friends all dropped by and gave him worthless advice, and poor old Job hung on, standing his ground and cleaving to his faith in God. The end to Job's story is one of greater prosperity, more children, and because he didn't give up, he was so blessed of God—the patience of Job. How many of us could go through all he did and come out victorious? Job had victory over grief and sorrow. Great patience was developed in Job's life as he sat in ashes and sackcloth.

Patience is enduring without murmuring, persevering with calmness. That seems to be such a tall order but one that must be kept. Patience has a work to do in us as we seek after it. Instilling it in our lives is another weapon to use against the devil. With patience we don't make hasty moves or decisions. "I waited patiently for the Lord; and he inclined unto me, and heard my cry" (Ps 40:1).

This psalm of David is beautiful as he speaks to the Lord, "Rest in the Lord, and wait patiently for him: fret not thyself because of him who prospereth in his way, because of the man who bringeth wicked devices to pass" (Ps 37:7). Devices are imaginations, inventions, vision, creativity, plan, provision, groundwork.

Rest and wait is helping us to regroup physically and mentally and to not get ahead of God's lead in our lives. Remember, the battle is his, not ours, and right in the middle of hot war and intense battle, we can rest and wait, building the patience up as faith is built by practicing or using frequently.

Instilling patience in daily living readies us for a later time when the enemy tries to throw a crisis at us or tries to bring disaster to our lives. Living in a touchy society nowadays brings forth 1 Peter 2:20, "For what glory is it if, when ye be buffeted for your faults, ye shall take it patiently? But if, when ye do well and suffer for it, ye take it patiently, this is acceptable with God."

Today it is full of lashing back when you've tried to help out and are only accused or put down for it. Extending a helping hand often gets it smacked. Being patient and calm is acceptable to God when this happens. It is a little hard at first, but not allowing offense to get in allows patience to flourish and grow. Being offended stops all growth, lets bitterness set in, lets in the devil. The most dangerous thing you can do is to be offended, to take offense. The enemy will snare you with it. Offense is a trap and is damaging to your well-being. The Lord has had to work with me on being offended. I enjoy helping, giving, and doing for others, and often I found myself being attacked, put down, and unappreciated. I finally understood the ploy of Satan and the verse of not getting weary of doing well. The Lord is patient.

"For so is the will of God, that with well doing ye may put to silence the ignorance of foolish men" (1 Pet. 2:15). I like this too. "And so, after he had patiently endured, he obtained the promise" (Heb 6:15).

Through faith, working with patience brings peace and rest amidst the storms and challenges of everyday life. As patience works, the wisdom of God comes to us. In God's wisdom is great counsel, answers, and directions. Paths are found to follow. God's wisdom is above man's wisdom and ways. The enemy wants you so distressed and upset that fear will take hold and freeze out all knowledge, and instead of victory, defeats wins.

Faith, patience, rest and peace, and God's counsel and wisdom are weapons against the devil that stalks after us. Using these tools as a way of life turns the tables, and the devil becomes the stalked prey, not us. He is the loser, not us.

The Word is full of God's wisdom and counsel for the people going against their enemies. Each recount has a different way God instructed them to fight. The children of Israel were many times outnumbered, but because they patiently waited on God's wisdom in their situation, they were overcomers, victorious winners. Saints get into trouble when they think God can't beat the devil out. We do not win by sight but by faith. You must get it down in your spirit that God can do all things; he has already whipped the enemy on Calvary and holds the keys. Now we as his children must take our places and realize who we are in Jesus and that we too have authority over the enemy in every area and aspect on this earth.

Patience keeps us free from the yoke of bandage. As children of God, we are liberated from what the world's lost are bound in. We are free, no more in bondage. "Standfast therefore in the liberty wherewith Christ hath made us free, and be not entangled again with the yoke of bondage" (Gal 5:1).

Chapter 2

Know the Enemy

Satan (Hebrew \say'tuhn\) means adversary, accuser, or slanderer. *Deceiver* is dissembler, liar, fast-talker, faker, imposter, serpent. *Enemy* is adversary, attacker, hostility, resistance, competitor, rival. *Evil* means mischief, nuisance, disaster, calamity, catastrophe, ruin, destruction. *Combatant* is fighter, litigant, soldier, warrior, assaulter, enemy. These are words and meanings that describe Satan, Lucifer, angel of light, the great deceiver.

Horror means fear, panic, anxiety. *Ridicule* is scoffing, mockery, gibes, taunts, sneer. *Discontent* means uneasiness, displeasure, restlessness, disconcert. These words are some of what Satan tries to do to us. Some of his ploys he works on us and in our lives.

Satan imitates the opposites of God. He brings evil; God brings good. He brings chaos; God brings peace. Satan enters with fear; God spreads joy and calm.

Satan set his eyes on the throne and wanted to be God. Satan is one of the mysterious figures of the Bible. The Old Testament tells the perception of him among the ancient people which changes over time. He rarely appears as a distinctive figure as in the New

Testament. Here is told of his wickedness, a being of great power and ruler of the demonic realm.

Among the Israelites, there was no conception of a personal supernatural force of absolute evil standing in opposition to God. On the supernatural level, the word *Satan* is first applied to an angel sent by God to withstand the Mesopotamian prophet Balaam who was hired by the king of Moab. The angel of the Lord took his stand in his way as his adversary (Satan) in Numbers 22:22. In three other places though, the supernatural adversary or accuser stands in opposition to good individuals and is more like the descriptions of Satan in the New Testament.

The Prophet Zechariah described a vision which he saw the High Priest Joshua standing trial before God for the sins of himself and the people, and Satan stood at his right hand to accuse him as a prosecutor would. Read in Zechariah 3:1–10 for the accounting of this.

Satan caused David to sin as he incited David to number Israel. Taking census was considered as an act of rebellion against God's sovereignty and for which Israel suffered great punishment. Look in 1 Chronicles 21:1–30 and then into the next chapter also.

By far the best known description of the enemy is in the Old Testament in the book of Job. The first two chapters find Satan the instrument of poor Job's suffering and agony.

> "Now there was a day when the sons of God came to present themselves before the Lord, and Satan came also among them" (Job 1:6).

Satan argued that Job worshipped because he was blessed with wealth; God gave permission, and the enemy destroyed all that Job loved and possessed. Then before the throne, the enemy again accused that Job had not suffered personal pain or physical pain. Again God gave permission.

> "So went Satan forth sent from the presence
> of the Lord, and smote Job with sore boils from
> the sole of his foot unto his crown" (Job 2:7).

Still Job would not sin against his God. Job knew nothing of the enemy's role in this affair. When the friends of Job entered, the role of Satan is not mentioned again, but we see that he acted within limits permitted by God. So the enemy has limits. I want to say that again. Satan has limits.

Near the beginning of the Christian era, writings began to contain descriptions of Satan that were much more varied and diabolic. The people became to understand their enemy as a ferocious figure, ruler of a vast demonic empire encompassing this world. They saw that it had become a battleground between good and evil, though God was Creator and would ultimately reclaim it for his own.

At the start of the ministry of Jesus, he had to confront the temptations for forty days and fasted in the wilderness. Satan challenged Jesus as the Son of God. He tempted Jesus to turn stones into bread for his own satisfaction and by leaping from the pinnacle of the temple, asking angels to bear him up. Touting, the devil even promised all the kingdoms of this world to Jesus if he would just bow down and worship him. Each time, Jesus turned Satan away by the Word. "And when the devil had ended all the temptation, he departed from him for a season" (Luke 4:13).

Through the New Testament, an awareness of continual warfare of Satan against the gospel is eminent. "Be sober, be vigilant; because your adversary the devil, as a roaring lion, walketh about, seeking whom he may devour" (1 Pet. 5:8).

The archenemy of the children of God does his job and uses every tactic to snare the Lord's beloved. But fear not, for though the evil and corruption reigns in the earth, the force of grace will prevail out.

> And there was war in heaven: Michael and
> his angels fought the dragon; and the dragon
> fought and his angels. And the great dragon was

cast out, that old serpent, called the Devil, and Satan, which deceiveth the whole world: he was cast out into the earth, and his angels were cast out with him. (Rev. 12:7–9)

Therefore rejoice, ye heavens, and ye that dwell in them. Woe to the inhabitants of the earth and of the sea! for the devil is come down unto you, having great wrath, because he knoweth that he hath but a short time. (Rev. 12:12)

And the dragon was wroth with the woman, and went to make war with the remnant of her seed, which keep the commandments of God, and have the testimony of Jesus Christ. (Rev. 12:17)

And the devil that deceived them was cast into the lake of fire and brimstone, where the beast and the false prophet are, and shall be tormented day and nite for ever and ever. (Rev. 20:10)

That is his end result, but in the meantime, we have to be of good cheer and be strong in the Lord for he *will* wage war on God's people.
Proverbs is a very favorite of mine. It holds wisdom and instruction and tells of warnings of evil and immorality.

Put away from thee a froward mouth, and perverse lips put far from thee. Turn not to the right hand nor to the left: remove thy foot from evil. (Prov. 4:24, 27)

These six things doth the Lord hate: yea, seven are an abomination unto him:

> A proud look, a lying tongue, and hands that shed innocent blood.
> An heart that deviseth wicked imaginations, feet that be swift in running to mischief,
> A false witness that speaketh lies, and he that soweth discord among brethren. (Prov. 6:16–19)

God says he hates these seven things. They are opposite of what he loves. These seven things are promoted by the devil, Satan, and he loves these things. His kingdom is built on these types of hateful things.

Just as faith is a spiritual force, so is fear a spiritual force and grief and sorrow. Fear, grief, and sorrow are spirits. Fear means dread, being afraid, distrust, and frightened. Sorrow and grief means the same—regret, lamentation, bemoaning, rue, heavy weight of emotion, loss.

Spirits of evil have names just as Satan has and God's angels do. Their intent is to torment God's children, do the work of Satan, and try to steal your mind and soul. Satan is their god and ruler. They have assignments to carry out against mankind and against God's people.

The Word speaks of demon possession and demons' names. Let's look at some of them to get a better picture at what we war against and the bondages they put on us.

> "Forasmuch then as the children are partakers of flesh and blood, he also himself likewise took part of the same; that through death he might destroy him that had the power of death, that is the devil; and deliver them who through fear of death were all their lifetime subject to bondage" (Heb 2:14–15).

The purpose of torment is to drive you to act on fear. Oppression is a spirit as well. Oppression is abuse, persecution, injury, depravity, brute force, infliction, and crush. The spirits of fear, grief, sorrow, and oppression try to take away man's goods by force and terror without having the right or authority by working on man's weakness and ignorance. To let these spirits control you is saying that Satan and they are bigger than God.

There are four divisions of evil spirits:

1. Principalities
2. Powers
3. Rulers of darkness
4. Wicked spirits in high places

> For we wrestle not against flesh and blood, but against principalities, against powers, against the rulers of the darkness of this world, against spiritual wickedness in high places. (Eph 6:12)

> And his fame went throughout all Syria: and they brought him all sick people that were taken with divers diseases and torments, and those which were possessed with devils, and those which were lunatick, and those that had the palsy; and he healed them. (Matt. 4:24)

Divers means difference, discrepancy, disparity, imbalance. Here you can see the variety Jesus was healing—the diseased, the possessed, the lunatic, the tormented, and the ones that had palsy.

"Many will say to me in that day, Lord, Lord, have we not prophesied in thy name? And in thy name have cast out devils? And in thy name done many wonderful works?" (Matt. 7:22). To cast out devils means possessed of body.

> "But the Pharisees said, He casteth out devils through the prince of the devils" (Matt. 9:34).

Here Jesus is accused of being a devil, casting out devils and by the name of Beelzebub, the prince of devils.

"Then was brought unto him one possessed with a devil, blind and dumb: and he healed him, insomuch that the blind and dumb both spake and saw" (Matt. 12:22).

This devil's name was Blind and Dumb. Jesus cast it out.

"And certain women, which had been healed of evil spirits and infirmities, Mary called Magdalene, out of whom went seven devils" (Luke 8:2).

These seven are not named but had names nonetheless.

Jesus was saying the people are of their father the devil. They will do the lusts of the devil. The devil is a murderer from the beginning. There is no truth in him. He is a liar and the father of lies (John 8:44).

"And that they may recover themselves out of the snare of the devil, who are taken captive by him at his will" (2 Tim. 2:26). Recover is to awake or arouse. We are to wake up and get out of the snare! Captive is being held hostage, bound, in bondage.

"Yea, and all that will live godly in Christ Jesus shall suffer persecution" (2 Tim. 3:12). Here it is! *All* who live godly lives in Jesus *will suffer* persecution, be attacked, gone after by the devil and his demons and be made war on.

> This know also, that in the last days perilous times shall come.
> For men shall be lovers of their own selves, covetous, boasters, proud, blasphemers, disobedient to parents, unthankful, unholy, without natural affection, trucebreakers, false accusers, incontinent, fierce, despisers of those that are good, traitors, heady, high minded, lovers of pleasures more than lovers of God. (2 Tim. 3:1–4)

This description sure sounds like what the world is today, and we are in the last days, folks. "But evil men and seducers shall wax worse and worse, deceiving, and being deceived" (2 Tim. 3:13).

Again, evil is rampant today and is just getting worse and worse. "For he said unto him, Come out of the man, thou unclean spirit. And he asked him, What is thy name? And he answered, saying, My name is Legion: for we are many" (Mark 5:8–9).

This demon's name was Legion because there were so many of them in this man, hundreds, perhaps thousands. Legion is multitudes, upward of, many, numerous. There are two thousand swine feeding nearby, and that legion of devils was allowed by Jesus to enter the pigs. The pigs ran down into the sea and drowned themselves (see Mark 5:12–13).

> "Behold, I have created the smith that bloweth the coals in an instrument for his work; and I have created the waster to destroy. No weapon that is formed against thee shall prosper; and every tongue that shall rise against thee in judgment thou shalt condemn. This is the heritage of the servants of the Lord, and their righteousness is of me, saith the Lord" (Is 54:16–17).

From God's point of view, we can stand against the enemy and all the ugliness he flings at us and tries to slip in on us. We have heritage. We stand in righteousness, two more weapons to defeat the lion with.

Blocking out the world's ways blocks out the world's junk, the devil's trash. Fear, perverseness, crimes, drug abuse—the list is too long. Living in the world's ways compromise and steals God's best for us from us. We are in the world but are not to be of the world.

In the ways of the lost world, Satan has to be received into our heart and be accepted to do any harm in us. If we don't receive and accept trouble when it comes knocking on the door, it can't enter in and is not received. Quit receiving the devil's junk as he peddles.

Fear stops faith if allowed in. Faith overcomes fear if faith dwells in the heart.

There are four more weapons.

1. Heritage
2. Righteousness
3. Standing on the Word
4. Not receiving untruths

Knowing this holds the enemy at bay, making it harder to enter in. You make a hedge to form around you, causing it harder for the enemy to get at you.

The Word covers us, clothes us. We wear it, speak it, walk in it, live in it. We have faith in it, hope in it, and become what it says we are. Use it, follow it, and do what it says. We are double covered in the spiritual which spills over into the flesh and covers us there as well. When we take care of the spiritual things, we are also taken care of in the natural.

> "But rather seek ye the kingdom of God; and all these things shall be added unto you" (Luke 12:31).

Following God brings to us double coverage: (1) covered in the spirit, (2) covered in the flesh.

> "Regard not them that have familiar spirits, neither seek after wizards, to be defiled by them: I am the Lord your God" (Lev. 19:31).

> "But the prince of the kingdom of Persia withstood me one and twenty days: but, lo, Michael, one of the chief princes, came to help me; and I remained there with the kings of Persia" (Dan. 10:13).

God had heard Daniel's prayer the first day and had sent an angel, Gabriel, but the enemy had sent his angel to stop the answer to prayer, and so the fight continued between the two angels until Michael, the first archangel of God, had to come and help battle the evil principality.

Evil principalities linger over nations and their leaders.

Daniel prayed, and God moved King Cyrus to rebuild Jerusalem and the temple.

> "That saith of Cyrus, He is my shepherd, and shall perform all my pleasure: even saying to Jerusalem, Thou shalt be built; and to the temple, Thy foundation shall be laid" (Is 44:28).

We have a part too in the angelic conflicts. When we pray for leaders of nations, we help establish what God's will is for that nation.

When we pray for people and their situations, we stand in the spirit against the enemies. So then the ranks of the enemies are

1. Lucifer, Satan, the devil,
2. Wickedness in high places—nations and rulers,
3. Rulers of darkness—nations,
4. Powers—attack leadership,
5. Principalities—attack everybody.

> I *exhort* therefore, that, first of all, supplications, prayers, intercessions, and giving of thanks, be made for all men; for kings, and for all that are in authority; that we may lead a quiet and peaceable life in all godliness and honesty. (1 Tim. 2:1–2)

> Yet Michael the archangel, when contending with the devil he disputed about the body of Moses, durst not bring against him a railing accusation, but said, The Lord rebuke Thee. (Jude 1:9)

Michael was very careful to rebuke the devil in the Lord.
The story of Gideon is in Judges 6:1–24. Now Gideon suffered from depression because of the awful circumstances. God sent an angel because his people had a need and not because they were all so spiritual. The angel called Gideon a mighty man of valor. The angel also told Gideon that he was to save Israel. So Gideon asked the angel for a sign, and fire came up from the rock to consume his sacrifice. Gideon was still depressed and said he was going to die, even after God had called him a deliverer. Gideon met Jehovah Shalom, the God of peace, and built another altar and offered another sacrifice. Gideon tore down the altar of Baal. Depression is the sin of unbelief and is a spirit like fear and grief as the others are too.

The story of Hezekiah is in 1 Chronicles 28–30, three chapters. Hezekiah was the son of an awful king, Ahaz. Ahaz sacrificed his children to a god named Molech. Well, Hezekiah was a godly king who opened, cleaned, and rededicated the temple and restored worship. Sennacherib, the king of Assyria, had already taken the northern kingdom into captivity and attacked Judah in the south. Now Isaiah, the prophet, and King Hezekiah stood fast and prayed. The Lord sent an angel to smite King Sennacherib. One hundred eighty-five thousand men were slain. The situation had been depressing, but God turned it around.

Jealousy is a spirit. Because of jealousy, there was a plan to destroy Daniel. Chapter 6 of Daniel covers him in the lion's den.

Daniel was favored and successful—a wise man, a courtier, an interpreter of dreams. The reign of Darius the Mede was when Daniel was around eighty years old. Daniel, being the most distinguished of the three presidents that directed the 120 governors that ruled the empire, was to be set up over all the kingdom. Thus enters jealousy. The Jewish courtier's preeminence made Daniel the object of envy. And Daniel's rivals made Darius sign an edict that no one could pray to any god or man but to Darius alone for thirty days or be cast into the den of lions. Once the document was signed, it couldn't be changed even by the king. So was the law of the Medes and Persians. In spite of the edict, he still prayed three times daily to his God before an open window facing Jerusalem. Immediately his rivals brought charges against him. Thus the plot was seen by the distraught king. The king had no choice but to put Daniel in the den. Sleepless, the king rushed to the den next morning to see Daniel unharmed. The Lord had sent an angel to protect him. The king vented on the rivals, and the lions were killed instantly. All now were to fear the Lord of Daniel.

> For I am persuaded, that neither death, nor life, nor angels, nor principalities, nor powers, nor things present, nor things to come, nor height, nor depth, nor any other creature, shall be able to separate us from the love of God, which is in Christ Jesus our Lord. (Rom 8:38–39)

> Lest Satan should get an advantage of us: for we are not. ignorant of his devices. (2 Cor 2:11)

> When the unclean spirit is gone out of a man, he walketh through dry places, seeking rest, and findeth none.
> Then he saith, I will return into my house from whence I came out; and when he is come, he findeth it empty, swept, and garnished.
> Then goeth he, and taketh with himself seven other spirits more wicked than himself, and they enter in and dwell there: and the last state of that man is worse than the first. Even so shall it be also unto this wicked generation. (Matt. 12:43–45)

Satan knows his time is short. In this time remaining, he will do what it takes to bring you down, wear you out, and go for the weakest parts of you and what you have. Every saint needs to know warfare and teach your children and grandchildren. Now that we have looked at who and what the enemies are, let's kick butt!

Chapter 3

Gotta Get Dressed

The Word of God is full of glory. The glory is the presence of God. *Glory* means celestial bliss, paradise, nirvana, aurora, flash, blaze, scintillation, reflection, splendor, effulgence.

> Then a cloud covered the tent of the congregation, and the glory of the Lord filled the tabernacle.
> And Moses was not able to enter into the tent of the congregation, because the cloud abode thereon, and the glory of the Lord filled the tabernacle.
> And when the cloud was taken up from over the tabernacle, the children of Israel went onward in all their journeys. (Ex 40:34–36)

Moses led the children, following the presence of the Lord, cloud by day and fire by night. When the cloud was taken up, they would move. If it didn't move, neither did they.

Being children ourselves, we should live as they did in God's presence all the time, letting him lead, moving only if he guides us, stopping when he stops, waiting on the Lord, watching only him.

Exodus 16:10 tells us that as Aaron spoke to all the children of Israel that they looked toward the wilderness and saw the glory of the Lord in the cloud.

The story goes on to tell how God spoke then to Moses, telling him that in the evening meat would be eaten and in the morning bread would be eaten and that they would know that he was the Lord their God. God sent quail for meat, and he sent a small round thing called *manna* for the bread.

The presence of God is over his people then and now. We are just as important to him as the Jews, his chosen.

Jesus gave us the glory.

> That thou art in me, and I in thee, that they also may be one in us: that the world may believe that thou hast sent me.
>
> And the glory which thou gavest me I have given them; that they may be one, even as we are one:
>
> I in them, and thou in me, that they may be made perfect in one; and that the world may know that thou hast sent me, and hast loved them, as thou hast loved me.
>
> Father, I will that they also, whom thou hast given me, be with me where I am; that they may behold my glory, which thou hast given me: for thou lovest me before the foundation of the world.
>
> And I have declared unto them thy name, and will declare it: that the love wherewith thou hast loved me may be in them and I in them. (John 17:21–24, 26)

This was only parts of the prayer that Jesus prayed before he was delivered by Judas into the hands of men and officers from the chief priests and Pharisees.

We have the love of God and of Jesus in us and the glory in us with them to be made one with them. What a weapon! The glory is revealed in us.

> The Spirit itself beareth witness with our spirit, that we are the children of God:
>
> And if children, then heirs; heirs of God, and joint heirs with Christ; if so be that we suffer with him, that we may be also glorified together.
>
> For I reckon that the sufferings of this present time are not worthy to be compared with the glory which shall be revealed in us. (Rom 8:16–18)

Having the glory in us does what then in us?

> But have renounced the hidden things of dishonesty, not walking in craftiness, nor handling the word of God deceitfully; but by manifestation of the truth commending ourselves to every man's conscience in the sight of God.
>
> But if our gospel be hid, it is hid to them that are lost:
>
> In whom the god of this world hath blinded the minds of them which believe not, lest the light of the glorious gospel of Christ, who is the image of God, should shine unto them.
>
> For we preach not ourselves, but Christ Jesus the Lord; and ourselves your servants for Jesus' sake.
>
> For God, who commanded the light to shine out of darkness, hath shined in our hearts,

to give the light of the knowledge of the glory of God in the face of Jesus Christ.
 But we have this treasure in earthen vessels, that the excellency of the power may be of God, and not of us. (2 Cor 4:2–7)

The glory gives us these things:

1. *Truth* is manifested in us.
2. *Things of Satan* are renounced in us.
3. The gospel is *hidden* in us.
4. Our heart *shines* with the light of Christ.
5. *Good news*, gospel, is preached to others and shared.
6. *Knowledge* of the glory is given to us.
7. *Power of God* in us, a treasure, is the glory.

While we experience all seven manifestations of the glory in our bodies as children of God, Paul goes on to tell more about what the glory and power in us does.

> We are troubled on every side, yet not distressed; we are perplexed; but not in despair;
> Persecuted, but not forsaken; cast down, but not destroyed;
> Always bearing about in the body the dying of the Lord Jesus, that the life also of Jesus might be made manifest in our body. (2 Cor 4:8–10)

The glory or presence of God in us and over us and around us prevents us from feeling and experiencing what the world feels and experiences. When we give God our problems of life, we are (1) troubled but *not* distressed, (2) perplexed but *not* despaired, (3) cast down but *not* destroyed.

If you notice, the lost, unsaved people of the world are distressed, despaired, and destroyed by Satan. God protects us from this happening. Sure, Satan brings bad situations and crisis to our lives, but the glory, presence of God blocks him from destroying us and from perplexing and distressing us.

The glory of God, his presence, gives us (1) power, (2) protection, (3) guidance, (4) oneness with God, (5) fullness with God's love. The glory is a treasure as it says in 2 Corinthians 4:7, "But we have this treasure in earthen vessels, that the excellency of the power may be of God, and not of us."

The Word is full of glory, the presence of God. The Word is alive. The gospels are our shoes of the armor we wear. The Word is part of the armor. The glory, presence of God, is in the Word which is alive and is a weapon to stand against the devil.

> The night is far spent, the day is at hand: let us therefore cast off the works of darkness, and let us put on the armor of light.
>
> Let us walk honestly, as in the day; not in rioting and drunkenness, not in chambering and wantonness, not in strife and envying.
>
> But put ye on the Lord Jesus Christ, and make not provision for the flesh, to fulfill the lusts thereof. (Rom 13:12–14)

Let us put the armor of light, put on Jesus. He is the armor of light. The glory gives us power to tread down the enemy and his wickedness.

> "And ye shall tread down the wicked; for they shall be ashes under the soles of your feet in the day that I shall do this, saith the Lord of hosts" (Mal 4:3).

Satan is ashes under our feet. We need to view him as such, and his sudden appearance against us will be put in perspective as we face our opponent.

> "Who coverest thyself with light as with a garment: who stretchest out the heavens like a curtain: Who maketh his angels spirits; his ministers a flaming fire" (Ps 104:2, 4).

The light is the glory. The flaming fire is the glory. God is the glory. "She shall give to thine head an ornament of grace: a crown of glory shall she deliver to thee" (Prov. 4:9). God's wisdom gives to us a crown, a crown of glory. It covers us as an ornament on our head of grace and glory. Grace means the favor of God, God's favorite, great favor, blessings.

> He taught. me also, and said unto me, let thine heart retain my words: keep my commandments, and live.
> Get wisdom, get understanding: forget it not; neither decline—from the words—of my mouth.
> Forsake her not, and she shall preserve thee: love her, and. she shall keep thee.
> Wisdom is the principal thing; therefore get wisdom: and with all thy getting get understanding. (Prv 4:4–7)

God gives us his wisdom and understanding. Earthly wisdoms and understandings are no good to us in fighting the devil. God's wisdom brings us to meditate in the Word. Meditating on God's Word builds in us the image of what we are and who we are in Jesus.

Satan works frantically to destroy that image that builds and grows in us. He tries to use five things to destroy the image in your heart: (1) affliction, (2) persecution, (3) cares of this world, (4) deceit in riches, (5) lusts in riches. Mark 4:14–19 tells of these five ways the enemy comes against us.

> "This book of the law shall not depart out of thy mouth; but thou shalt meditate therein

day and night, that thou mayest observe to do according to all that is written therein: for then thou shalt make thy way prosperous, and then thou shalt have good success" (Josh 1:8).

We are to meditate day and night on the Word and do all that it says. Our way will be prosperous, and we will have success. We will also build the image of God up in us and who we are and what we are in him:

1. The Word is our contact with God.
2. Our minds are renewed by the Word.
3. We are indwelled by the Word.
4. The Word builds us.
5. Faith comes by the Word.

"So then faith cometh by hearing, and hearing by the word of God" (Rom 10:17). "Then said the Lord unto me, Thou hast well seen: for I will hasten my word to perform it" (Jer 1:12).

God watches over his Word to perform it. No weapon formed against us will prosper. The Word is alive. It is a living thing, and nothing is hidden from its view. The Word is settled forever in heaven. "Forever, O Lord, thy word is settled in heaven" (Ps 119:89).

Living by the Word (1) brings approval of God. (2) We are in agreement with him. (3) God's wisdom is imparted to us. (4) It brings us into who and what we are in him. 5) We are protected with a hedge roundabout us.

Living by the Word is living by faith:

1. Put the Word first.
2. Meditate on the Word.
3. Agree with what the Word says.
4. Act on the Word.
5. Speak the Word.

You will see your circumstances start turning around and changing. You'll be putting these weapons to use. These five actions is called *revelation knowledge*.

The Word is the sword of the spirit. It gives protection and victory. Without the living Word in our lives, Satan will try to take way our heir privileges: (1) success, (2) healing, (3) prosperity, (4) authority.

> But what saith it? The word is nigh thee, even in thy mouth, and in thy heart: that is, the word of faith, which we preach. (Rom 10:8)

> For if any be a hearer of the word, and not a doer, he is like unto a man beholding his natural face in a glass:
> For he beholdeth himself, and goeth his way, and straightway forgetteth what manner of man he was.
> But whoso looketh into the perfect law of liberty, and continueth therein, he being not a forgetful hearer, but a doer of the work, this man shall be blessed in his deed. (Jas 1:23–25)

Action of the Word is released in two ways: (1) through the words of your mouth, (2) through your actions. Satan brings doubt. Doubt is a thief. We stop the action and motion of the living Word when we let doubt creep in, whether it is doubt in heart or in confession.

> "And immediately Jesus stretched forth his hand, and caught him, and said unto him, O thou of little faith, wherefore didst thou doubt?" (Matt. 14:31)

Peter was literally walking on the water to meet Jesus coming at them as he walked on the water. But then doubt seized Peter when he realized what he really was doing, and he suddenly sank. By faith, Peter stepped out onto the water and walked; by doubt, Peter then sank, and Jesus caught him.

Defeat the enemy by the Word:

1. Glory—indwelling spirit of God.
2. Speaking the Word.
3. Action—applying the Word.

> "That at that time ye were without Christ, being aliens from the commonwealth of Israel, and strangers from the covenants of promise, having no hope, and without God in the world" (Eph 2:12).

Without the Word in any trial or storm is to be without God. The Word is the power of God and puts us, the believers, in control.

> "For I am not ashamed of the gospel of Christ: for it is the power of God unto salvation to everyone that believeth; to the Jew first, and also to the Greek. For therein is the righteousness of God revealed from faith to faith: as it is written, The just shall live by faith" (Rom 1:16–17).

We are to live having faith in the Word, the power of god. In doing this, it undermines Satan and his traps and gives us the victory over him.

As doubt is used by the enemy against us, so is division and strife. If Satan can get you into division and strife, he cuts off the life of the Word and the power of the Word to you. He stops the entering of these in you (1 John 2:9–12 and Eph 4:18).

Get it settled down in your heart and soul that God is in control over everything, even Satan (yes, even him). He is only allowed to do what God lets him do. Even Satan has boundaries and limits.

> The wicked plotteth against the just, and gnasheth upon him with his teeth.
> The Lord shall laugh at him: for he seeth that his day is coming.
> The wicked have drawn out the sword, and have bent their bow, to cast down the poor and needy, and to slay such as be of upright conversation.
> Their sword shall enter into their own heart, and their bows shall be broken. (Ps 37:12–15)

Second Corinthians 9:6–11 and Philippians 4:10–19 say that God will supply all our needs and enrich us in all things. God is in control. Satan is *not* in control of the child of God. Here are four impulses you are ruled by: (1) faith or fear, (2) abundance or lack, (3) power or weakness, (4) healing or sickness. Which sounds the best? It's the four impulses of God, of course. That is why the Word-ruled mind is dominated by God's thoughts and ways, not by Satan's. His thoughts and ways are the opposite. The world lives by the flesh and then dies. We live by the Spirit and life. We have the mind of Christ.

> "For who hath known the mind of the Lord, that he may instruct him? But we have the mind of Christ" (1 Cor 2:16).

To be carnal minded is death, but being spiritual minded is life and peace (Prov. 3:2 and Rom 8:6).

The Word sees the whole thing both in the natural realm and in the spiritual realm. The Word sees the heart of men.

> For the word of God is quick, and powerful, and sharper than any twoedged sword, piercing even the dividing asunder of soul and spirit, and of the joints and marrow, and is a discerner of the thoughts and intents of the heart. (Heb 4:12)

> But God hath revealed them unto us by his Spirit: for the Spirit searcheth all things, yea, the deep things of God. (1 Cor 2:10)

> And be not conformed to this world: but be ye transformed by the renewing of your mind, that ye may prove what is that good, and acceptable, and perfect, will of God. (Rom 12:2)

> And he that searcheth the hearts knoweth what is the mind of the Spirit, because he maketh intercession for the saints according to the will of God. (Rom 8:27)

Don't be moved by what you see or hear:

1. Stay in faith.
2. Be grounded and rooted.
3. Know that God is in control.
4. Be victors and champions.

Get a winner's attitude. Decide from the Word that you won't be defeated and you're not going to be a quitter. Resist Satan and his thoughts and ways. There is God holding out to you in a much better way and life. Take it. Put your attention on God and his Word. Take your stand and don't budge. Settle it in your mind, heart, and soul that you're the winner, and you already are a winner before you even pick up the weapons of warfare.

The glory of God is in us, around us, over us in his presence, his covering, his clothing, his favor, and his grace. Greater is he that is in me than he that is in the world!

Chapter 4

True Weapons

Impatience gets us out of the liberty and freedom that Jesus delivered us from. It gets us out of the line of God's will for us and often costs us the battle. Impatience is not a good place for the child of God to be in. The world is very impatient nowadays. It tries to hurry and stress you out to where you have no manners, thoughts of the next person, or what it is doing to you physically and mentally. The impatience of the world is so deep that people are yelling at microwaves to hurry up! Impatience is hurrying people up to get to the red-light signal to sit and wait. It is pitiful, and God's people have no business partaking in this strife. People are so stressed out; they think they are calm and in control. Patience gives us strength. It gives us six developing strengths:

1. Teaches us to wait on direction.
2. Keeps us free from bondage.
3. Strengthens our faith to hold our position to believe until it comes to pass.
4. Brings rest and peace in the storm.
5. Keeps our eyes on Jesus.

6. Blocks being offended.

> "This I say then, Walk in the Spirit, and ye shall not fulfill the lust of the flesh" (Gal 5:16).

To walk in the Spirit is using our faith and patience. This protects us from living in the flesh and of the world. We grow in the Spirit as we put down the cry of the flesh.

> "And let us not be weary in well doing: for in due season we shall reap, if we faint not. As we have therefore opportunity, let us do good unto all men, especially unto them who are of the household of faith" (Gal 6:9–10).

To keep doing good unto all men, exercising our patience intertwines in our growth. In faith and patience, love is developed.

The cares of this world chokes out the Word if not guarded. That is why meditation in the Word protects your faith, patience, and love. They flourish and grow. Without the daily Word, the enemy will steal away all the beginning growth in these areas. He knows these are weapons and doesn't want them developed to be used against him.

The biggest mistake a Christian can make is to believe this is just a story or a myth. The other mistake is to think that he won't come after you or your family. To know something of your enemy gives an edge to the situation. I want to talk about the weapons we have in the fruits of the Spirit:

1. Love
2. Joy
3. Peace
4. Long-suffering
5. Gentleness
6. Goodness
7. Faith

8. Meekness
9. Temperance

I will take each one separately and find the weapons in each one.

Love

Living the love of Jesus is what we are all about. It's to be like him. Flexing the love levels to maturity is not fun but has to be accomplished. Just as faith and patience is practiced, so does the love area need to be developed. Loving the enemies in our life is a weapon to be used against the enemy. Love conquerors all. Love can't fuss or be in strife. Love covers a multitude of sins. Love develops discretion. The devil hates and destroys; we love and build. Love is a weapon the devil despises. If he can get us out of love and not love, it opens the door for strife, sin, bitterness, unforgiveness, backsliding, and the list goes on and on. It isn't easy to love an enemy, but we have to be an overcomer and do it.

By loving a person that hates you, you'll be free from bonds of hate, free from sin and free to grow and mature. To love your enemy is to do good to them, heaping coals of fire on their heads. Love frees you to really learn to love as Jesus does. Love becomes such a powerhouse of force as does faith and patience. Faith, patience, and love becomes a three-fold cord that is not easily broken. Your life will be dramatically changed when you allow your spirit to take over, leaving the flesh behind.

"Follow after charity, and desire spiritual gifts, but rather that ye may prophesy. But he that prophesieth speaketh unto men to edification, and exhortation, and comfort" (1 Cor 14:1, 3). We are to follow after love and desire spiritual gifts.

"For the love of Christ constraineth us; because we thus judge, that if one died for all, then were all dead" (2 Cor 5:14). The love of Jesus controls us.

Ye that love the Lord, hate evil: he preserveth the souls of his saints; he delivereth them out of the hand of the wicked. (Ps 97:10)

Pray for the peace of Jerusalem: they shall prosper that love thee. (Ps 122:6)

I love them that love me; and those that seek me early shall find me. (Prov. 8:17)

That I may cause those that love me to inherit substance; and I will fill their treasures. (Prov. 8:21)

Thou shalt not avenge, nor bear any grudge against the children of thy people, but thou shalt love thy neighbor as thyself: I am the Lord. (Lev. 19:18)

Hatred stirreth up strifes: but love covereth all sins. (Prov. 10:12)

A friend loveth at all times, and a brother is born for adversity. (Prov. 17:17)

But I say unto you, Love your enemies, bless them that curse you, do good to them that hate you, and pray for them which despitefully use you, and persecute you;
For if ye love them which love you, what reward have ye? do not the publicans the same? (Matt. 5:44, 46)

But the fruit of the Spirit is love, joy, peace, longsuffering, gentleness, goodness, faith, meekness, temperance: against such there is no law. (Gal 5:22–23)

There are so many scriptures on love. I think you get the point.

Joy

Then he said unto them, Go your way, eat the fat, and drink the sweet, and send portions unto them for whom nothing is prepared: for this day is holy unto our Lord: neither be ye sorry; for the joy of the Lord is your strength. (Neh 8:10)

Now the God of hope fill you with all joy and peace in believing, that ye may abound in hope, through the power of the Holy Ghost. (Rom 15:13)

Thou wilt shew me the path of life: in thy presence is fulness of joy; at thy right hand there are pleasures for ever more. (Ps 16:11)

For his anger endureth but a moment; in his favour is life: weeping may endure for a night, but joy cometh in the morning. (Ps 30:5)

They that sow in tears shall reap in joy. (Ps 126:5)

Therefore with joy shall ye water out the wells of salvation. (Is 12:3)

To appoint unto them that mourn Zion, to give unto them beauty for ashes, the oil of joy for mourning the garment of praise for the spirit of heaviness; that they might be called trees of righteousness, the planting of the Lord, that he might be glorified. (Is 61:3)

My brethren, count it all joy when ye fall into divers temptations. (Jas 1:2)

I have no greater joy than to hear that my children walk in truth. (3 Jn 1:4)

But rejoice, inasmuch as ye are partakers. of Christ's sufferings; that when his glory shall revealed, ye may be glad also with exceeding joy. (1 Peter 4:13)

Looking unto Jesus the author and finisher of our faith; who for the joy that was set before him endured the cross, despising the shame, and is set down at the right hand of the throne of God. (Heb 12:2)

For ye are our glory and joy. (1 Thes 2:20)

Again, there are so many scriptures on joy. We can have joy in the storm and keep right on going. To the world, they wonder why we are so glad while the battle rages on. It goes beyond their understanding how love, joy, peace, and the other fruits work in us.

Peace

Wherefore, beloved; seeing. that ye look for such things, be diligent that ye may be found of him in peace, without spot, and blameless. (2 Peter 3:14)

I will both lay me down in peace, and sleep: for thou, Lord, only makest me dwell in safety. (Ps 4:8)

The Lord will give strength unto his people; the Lard will bless his people with peace. (Ps 29:11)

Now the Lord of peace himself give you peace always by all means. The Lord be with you all. (2 Thes 3:16)

And to esteem them very highly in love for their work's sake. And be at peace among yourselves. (1 Thes 5:13)

For he is our peace, who hath made both one., and hath broken down the middle wall partition between us. (Eph 2:14)

Endeavouring to keep the unity of the Spirit in the bond of peace. (Eph 4:3)

Long-suffering

In the verses for this, I found none that directly says long-suffering, but I do feel it is connected with healing and sickness because when you go through the battles of sickness, you sometimes are in long-suffering for the healing to manifest and come. So the verses I give are on healing and sickness.

But he was wounded for our transgressions, he was bruised for our iniquities: the chastisement of our peace was upon him; and with his stripes we are healed. (Is 53:5)

For I will restore health unto thee, and I will heal thee of thy wounds, saith the Lord. (Jer 30:17)

The Lord is good, a strong hold in the day of trouble; and he knoweth them that trust in him. (Nahum 1:7)

Thou art my hiding place; thou shalt compass me about with songs of deliverance. (Ps 32:7)

Though he fall, he shall not be utterly cast down: for the Lord upholdeth him with his hand. (Ps 37:24)

Thou, which hast shewed me great and sore troubles, shalt quicken me again, and shalt bring me up again from the depths of the earth. (Ps 71:20)

Enduring a burden is long-suffering. Being in a situation that takes a lot of patience and time is long-suffering. There are many scriptures for each of the areas.

Gentleness

But we were gentle among you, even as a nurse cherisheth her children. (1 Thes 2:7)

But the wisdom that is from above is first pure, then peaceable, gentle, and easy to be intreated of, full of mercy and good fruits, without partiality, and without hypocrisy. (Jas 3:17)

Servants, be subject to your masters with all fear; not only to the good and gentle, but also to the froward. (1 Peter 2:18)

Now I Paul myself beseech you by the meekness and gentleness of Christ, who in presence am base among you, but being absent am bold toward you. (2 Cor 10:1)

Thou hast also given me the shield of thy salvation: and thy gentleness hath made me great. (2 Sam. 22:36)

To speak evil of no man, to be no brawlers, but gentle, shewing all meekness unto all men. (Titus 3:2)

Goodness

"Behold therefore the goodness and severity of God: on them which fell, severity; but toward thee, goodness, if thou continue in his goodness: otherwise thou shalt be cut off" (Rom 11:22).

"Or despisest thou the riches of his goodness and forbearance and longsuffering; not knowing that the goodness of God leadeth thee to repentance?" (Rom 2:4).

Long-suffering is used in this scripture.

Thou crownest the year with thy goodness; and thy paths drop fatness. (Ps 65:11)

Why boastest thou thyself in mischief, o mighty man? the goodness of God endureth continually. (Ps 52:1)

He loveth righteousness and judgment: the earth is full of goodness of the Lord. (Ps 33:5)

Oh how great is thy goodness, which thou hast laid up for them that fear thee; which thou hast wrought for them that trust in thee before the sons of men! (Ps 31:19)

I had fainted, unless I had believed to see the goodness of the Lord in the land of the living. (Ps 27:13)

Surely goodness and mercy shall follow me all the days of my life: and I will dwell in the house of the Lord forever. (Ps 23:6)

Faith is covered in length in chapter 1.

Meekness

The meek will he guide in judgment: and the meek will he teach his way. (Ps 25:9)

Blessed are the meek: for they shall inherit the earth. (Matt. 5:5)

But with righteousness shall he judge the poor, and reprove with equity for the meek of the earth. (Is 11:4)

The meek shall eat and be satisfied: they shall praise the Lord that seek him: your heart shall live forever. (Ps 22:26)

For the Lord taketh pleasure in his people: he will beautify the meek with salvation. (Ps 149:4)

The meek also shall increase their joy in the Lord, and the poor among men shall rejoice in the Holy One of Israel. (Is 29:19)

The Lord lifteth up the meek: he casteth the wicked down to the ground. (Ps 147:6)

A soft answer turneth away wrath: but grievous words stir up anger. (Prov. 15:1)

Temperance

Last but not least is temperance, which means self-control, moderation, sobriety, calmness.

Wherefore it shall come to pass, if ye hearken to these judgments, and keep, and do them, that the Lord thy God shall keep unto thee the covenant and the mercy which he sware unto thy fathers. (Deut. 7:12)

Therefore whosoever heareth these sayings of mine, and doeth them, I will liken him unto a wise man, which built his house upon a rock:
And the rain descended, and the floods came, and the winds blew, and beat upon that

> house; and it fell not; for it was founded upon a rock. (Matt. 7:24–25)

> If they obey and serve him, they shall spend their days in prosperity, and their years in pleasures. (Job 36:11)

So are the fruits of the spirit which we are called to produce in our lives. They are also weapons against the enemy, the devil.

There are also gifts of the Spirit:

1. Word of wisdom
2. Word of knowledge
3. Faith
4. Healing
5. Miracles
6. Prophecy
7. Discernment
8. Tongues
9. Interpretation of tongues

First Corinthians 12:8–10 lists the gifts of the Holy Spirit. We have already covered faith. Discernment of spirits is interesting and is used in warfare. This gift means a supernatural insight into the world of the spirit realm.

There are four things a Christian can discern:

1. The Holy Spirit (John 1:32–34)
2. Good angels (Acts 12:1–11)
3. Evil angels (Acts 16:16–18)
4. Human spirits (Luke 9:53–55)

Hebrews 5:14 tells you how to discern one or more of these spirits. Training your senses to discern is like training on faith; you exercise it. It will help you to know what spirit you're dealing with. "But strong meat belongeth to them that are of full age, even those who by reason of use have their senses exercised to discern both good and evil" (Heb 5:14).

All the gifts of the Spirit are to be used as are the fruits. I personally do not have all the gifts per se, and I don't know of anyone that does have them all, but I'm sure that there may be a few people out there. But whatever the gifts are that you do have, use them. Ask God if there are some you desire and believe he will send them.

These are more weapons to go against Satan with. The fruits and gifts go hand in hand and are used together at times such as love and miracles, discernment and tongues, prophesy and goodness.

> Wherefore I put thee in remembrance that thou stir up the gift of God, which is in thee by the putting on of many hands.
>
> For God hath not given us the spirit of fear; but of power, and of love, and of a sound mind.
>
> For the which cause I also suffer these things: nevertheless I am not ashamed: for I know whom I have believed., and am persuaded that he is able to keep that which I have committed unto him against that day. (2 Tim. 1:6–7, 12)

Chapter 5

Prepare for War

Warfare means contest, battle of good and evil. Which will prevail in your life and home? Will you go to battle against the enemy to protect your soul and family?

> For though we walk in the flesh, we do not war after the flesh:
> For the weapons of our warfare are not carnal, but mighty through God to the pulling down of strong holds;
> Casting down imaginations, and every high thing that exalteth itself against the knowledge of God, and bringing into captivity every thought to the obedience of Christ. (2 Cor 10:3–5)

Ephesians 6:10–18 is of putting on the armor of God, the whole armor, so you can stand against the wiles of the devil. Armor is used for battle and war. This is a battle for your soul, and your enemy, Satan, will take it any way he can. He hates God, and he hates you. He is not your friend, and he means you harm. This armor is designed to protect you, and if you notice, it covers only the front, not the back. The Lord guards the back. There is no place in the army of God for a coward. You are a devil stomper, a mighty warrior of the army of the Almighty, a Word-filled soldier.

> The night is far spent, the day is at hand: let us therefore cast off the works of darkness, and let us put on the armour of light.
> Let us walk honestly, as in the day; not in rioting and drunkenness, not in chambering and wantonness, not in strife and envying.
> But put ye on the Lord Jesus Christ, and make not provision for the flesh, to fulfill the lusts thereof. (Rom 13:12–14)

As we see, the armor of light is put on. Jesus is that armor. We are to walk in honesty. This battle of war is not of flesh but of spirit, and we cannot win if we prepare in the flesh. The armor of the spirit is different than armor of the body.

> "By the word of truth, by the power of God, by the armour of righteousness on the right hand and on the left" (2 Cor 6:7).

Righteousness means being upright before God. As we are to put on Jesus as armor, we are to put on righteousness as armor too. Now let's examine the armor of the Spirit we are to put on and use.

> Put on the whole armour of God, that ye may be able to stand against the wiles of the devil.
> For we wrestle not against flesh and blood, but against principalities, against powers, against the rulers of the darkness of this world, against spiritual wicked ness in high places.

Wherefore take unto you the whole armour of God, that ye may withstand in the evil day, and having done all, to stand.
Stand therefore, having your loins girt about with truth., and having on the breastplate of righteousness;
And your feet shod with the preparation of the gospel of peace;
Above all, taking the shield of faith, wherewith ye shall be able to quench all fiery darts of the wicked.
And take the helmet of salvation, and the sword of the Spirit, which is the word of God. (Eph 6:11–17)

This is the armor we are to put on and walk in every day, all day in the Christian walk. This armor protects us. It totally covers us from head to toe in the front. God himself covers our back.

Let's break down each one of the verses to each piece of the armor and how to apply it. Here are the six parts of the armor:

"Stand therefore, having your loins girt about with truth, and having on the breastplate of righteousness" (Eph 6:14)

1. Stay in the Word.
   "Loins girt about with truth" means to stay in the Word. It is truth and shows you the answer for every situation.
2. Walk in Jesus kind of love.
   "Breastplate of righteousness" means to walk in the love of Jesus in all circumstances.

"And your feet shod with the preparation of the gospel of peace" (Eph 6:15).

3. Speak peace.
"Feet shod with the preparation of the gospel of peace" means to be filled with the Word to speak peace on all occasions.

"Above all, taking the shield of faith, wherewith ye shall be able to quench all the fiery darts of the wicked" (Eph 6:16).

4. Use faith and believe.
"Shield of faith" means using faith and believing you have the victory at every turn against the devil.

"And the helmet of salvation, and the sword of the spirit, which is the word of God" (Eph 6:17).

5. Hope in Jesus.
"Helmet of salvation" means hope in Jesus through all things.

6. The Word stands.
"Sword of the spirit" means the Word of God stands against all evil.

Stay in the Word, walk in the love of Jesus, speak peace, use your faith and believe, have hope in Jesus, know the Word stands. These are the six parts of our daily armor we are to put on along with putting on Jesus and his righteousness.

There are three kinds of armor:

1. Jesus is the armor of light (Rom 13:12–14).
2. Righteousness is armor (2 Cor 6:7).
3. Six-part spiritual armor (Eph 6:14–17).

If we do all that is required, Satan does not know it is us in the armor and not God. We are covered, and if we walk in what is the knowledge given us, the devil thinks it is the Lord he is up against, not us. It is a strategy of God against his enemy in warfare against us, his children.

We are to cast down imaginations and every high thing that exalts itself against the knowledge of God. We are to bring into captivity every thought to the obedience of Christ. We are not to be moved by what we see but be moved by what the Word says. The gospel is the power of God entrusted to us.

> For I am not ashamed of the gospel of Christ: for it is the power of God unto salvation to everyone that believeth; to the Jew first, and also to the Greek.
>
> For therein is the righteousness of God revealed from faith to faith: as it is written, The just shall live by faith. (Rom 1:16–17)

> According to the glorious gospel of the blessed God, which was committed to my trust. (1 Tim. 1:11)

> But as we were allowed of God to be put in trust with the gospel, even so we speak; not as pleasing men, but God, which trieth our hearts. (1 Thes 2:4)

> The name of the Lord is a strong tower: the righteous runneth into it, and is safe. (Prov. 18:10)

Peter became an example of the struggle of faith and understanding that every disciple faces. His difficulty with the lessons Jesus had to teach him continued to the end of Jesus's life. By the time of the Last Supper, Peter had steeled himself to the dangers that Jesus had predicted. After the crucifixion, Peter emphasized Jesus's knowledge when he said three times to Jesus, "Yes, Lord, you know that I love you." Jesus commissioned Peter to feed his sheep (Jn 21:15–17). Peter would die for his master. Through his own weakness and cowardice, he had been restored through the mystery of the resurrection of Jesus as we too are. We have the authority to use the name of Jesus. In Acts 3:1–12, Peter uses the power in the name of Jesus.

> Now Peter and John went up together into the temple at the hour of prayer, being the ninth hour.
>
> And a certain man lame from his mother's womb was carried, whom they laid daily at the gate of the temple which is called Beautiful, to ask alms of them that entered into the temple;
>
> Who seeing Peter and John about to go into the temple asked an alms.
>
> And Peter, fastening his eyes upon him with John, said, Look on us.
>
> And he gave heed unto them, expecting to receive something of them.
>
> Then Peter said, Silver and gold have I none; but such as I have give I thee: In the name of Jesus Christ of Nazareth rise up and walk.
>
> And he took him by the right hand, and lifted him up: and immediately his feet and ankle bones received strength.
>
> And he leaping up stood, and walked, and entered with them into the temple, walking, and leaping, and praising God.
>
> And all the people saw him walking and praising God:
>
> And they knew that it was he which sat for alms at the Beautiful gate of the temple: and they were filled with wonder and amazement at that which happened unto him.

And as the lame man which was healed held Peter and John, all the people ran together unto them in the porch that is called Solomon's, greatly wondering,

And when Peter saw it, he answered unto the people, Ye men of Israel, why marvel ye at this? or why look ye so earnestly on us, as though by our own power or holiness we had made this man to walk? (Acts 3:1–12)

Then Peter, filled with the Holy Ghost, said unto them, Ye rulers of the people, and elders of Israel,

If we this day be examined of the good deed done to the impotent man, by what means he is made whole;

Be it known unto you all, and to all the people of Israel that by the name of Jesus Christ of Nazareth, whom ye crucified, whom God raised from the dead, even by him doth this man stand here before you whole. (Acts 4:8–10)

The name of Jesus is a weapon for us to use. His name overcomes the darkness and ruler of this world we live in. His name is authority over all. His name commands that all bow before him. His name is given to us to use.

"And I will give unto thee the keys of the kingdom of heaven: and whatsoever thou shalt bind on earth shall be bound in heaven: and whatsoever thou shalt loose on earth shall be loose in heaven" (Matt. 16:19).

There are two keys: (1) bind, (2) loose. What we bind or loose here on earth in Jesus's name is bound and loosed in heaven, two more weapons to use against the adversary, the devil.

God has given us many weapons of war to use against Satan. We must know them on how to use them. We must have faith in our weapons. The weapons of God will work, and the Word fights its own battles. We are to be good soldiers, men and women of faith. Our weapons of warfare are mighty through God.

> For though we walk in the flesh, we do not war after the flesh:
> (For the weapons of our warfare are not carnal, but mighty through God to the pulling down of strong holds;)
> Casting down imaginations, and every high thing that exalteth itself against the knowledge of God, and bringing into captivity every thought to the obedience of Christ;
> And having in a readiness to revenge all disobedience, when your obedience is fulfilled. (2 Cor 10:3–6)

God is moved by our faith. "Seeing then that we have a great high priest, that is passed into the heavens, Jesus the Son of God, let us hold fast our profession. For we have not an high priest which cannot be touched with the feeling of our infirmities; but was in all points tempted like as we are, yet without sin" (Heb 4:14–15).

God has provided us with four undefeatable answers:

1. The written Word
2. The blood of Jesus
3. The name of Jesus
4. The Holy Spirit

Satan has no authority over the body of Christ's children. Don't let him have what is yours.

It is difficult to walk this walk of God that we are called to without allowing our feelings and emotions to get involved, but we mustn't allow this to enter. Satan plays on our feelings and emotions and wants you to let them rule instead of faith and the Word. To live by faith puts how we feel and if we think it is fair down in its place. Living by faith overrides the emotional roller coaster. Putting the Word into first place settles things and puts the emotions second in line. Practice does make perfect on this just as it does on all the other things we have covered.

We mature by becoming skillful in the Word, applying the Word, and living the Word.

> For every one that useth milk is unskillful in the word of righteousness: for he is a babe.
> But strong meat belongeth to them that are of full age, even those who by reason of use have their senses exercised to discern both good and evil. (Heb 5:13–14)

> That we henceforth be no more children, tossed to and fro, and carried about with every wind of doctrine, by the sleight of men, and cunning craftiness, whereby they lie in wait to deceive;
> But speaking the truth in love, may grow up into him in all things, which is the head, even Christ:
> From whom the whole body fitly joined together and compacted by that which every joint supplieth, according to the effectual working in the measure of every part, maketh increase of the body unto the edifying of itself in love.
> That ye put off concerning the former conversation the old man, which is corrupt according to the deceitful lusts;
> And be renewed in the spirit of your mind;

And that ye put on the new man, which after God is created in righteousness and true holiness. (Eph 4:14–16, 22–24)

The way of the Lord is strength to the upright but destruction shall be to the workers of iniquity. (Prov. 10:29)

Chapter 6

Use of the Unexpected

Shortly after leaving Egypt, the Lord's might had been dramatically demonstrated when the people were attacked by a fierce desert tribe, the Amalekites. Under the leadership of Moses's aide-de-camp Joshua, the Hebrews fought back. They dominated the battle as long as Moses, observing from the crest of a nearby hill, held his hands stretched out. When his energy waned and his arms dropped, the tide of the battle turned. Finally, Moses sat on a huge rock, and others supported his outstretched arms until sunset by which time Joshua had finally achieved the victory.

> Then came Amalek, and fought with Israel in Rephidim.
> And Moses said unto Joshua, Choose us out men, and go out, fight with Amalek: tomorrow I will stand on the top of the hill with the rod of God in mine hand.
> So Joshua did as Moses had said to him, and fought with Amalek: and Moses, Aaron, and Hur went up to the top of the hill.

And it came to pass, when Moses held up his hand, that Israel prevailed: and when he let down his hand, Amalek prevailed.

But Moses's hands were heavy; and they took a stone, and put it under him, and he sat thereon; and Aaron and Hur stayed up his hands, the one on the one side, and the other on the other side; and his hands were steady until the going down of the sun.

And Joshua discomforted Amalek and his people with the edge of the sword.

And the Lord said unto Moses, Write this for a memorial in a book, and rehearse it in the ears of Joshua: for I will utterly put out the remembrance of Amalek from under heaven.

And Moses built an altar, and called the name of it Jehovahnissi:

For he said, Because the Lord hath sworn that the Lord will have war with Amalek from generation to generation. (Ex 17:8–16)

So was the might of the Lord seen by Moses obeying and instructing the people. In obeying, Moses held forth his hands with the rod of God over the battle. Moses could have said that he would look dumb on the hill doing this and he didn't want to be embarrassed. Moses could've said no to God's instructions, but as odd as they were, Moses followed them, and the victory was won.

Has God instructed you in a peculiar way? Did he ask you to do something out of the ordinary in a circumstance? Did the Lord direct you in a direction that you felt was offbeat? Did you obey? Or did you reason with your head and not follow his instructions? Often our battles are lost because we don't obey God. We don't trust him to know what we need to do. We don't like unusual ways, do we? But we have to remember that God's ways are above our ways, and his ways are not our ways. We are shortsighted. He sees clear to the end of things and knows what is needed. He can't move on our behalf if we don't listen, obey, and carry out what he tells us.

Have you ever listened to old war stories? The battles are not won when the troops don't carry out the officers' instructions. The men that allow fear to seize them don't obey the orders and turn tail and run, which costs the fellow men the victory. At times, ground was lost due to deserters. Other times, missions were abandoned because of someone not being where they were needed at a crucial time.

> Behold, I set before you this day a blessing and a curse;
> A blessing, if ye obey the commandments of the Lord your God, which I command you this day:
> And a curse, if ye will not obey the commandments of the Lord your God, but turn aside out of the way which I command you this day, to go after other gods, which ye have not known. (Deut. 11:26–28)

> And Samuel said, Hath the Lord as great delight in burnt offerings and sacrifices, as in obeying the voice of the Lord? Behold, to obey is better than sacrifice, and to hearken than the fat of rams. (1 Sam. 15:22)

> Saying, did not we straitly command you that ye should not teach in this name? and, behold, ye have filled Jerusalem with your doctrine, and intend to bring this man's blood upon us.
> Then Peter and the other apostles answered and said, We ought to obey God rather than men. (Acts 5:28–29)

> But this thing commanded I them, saying, Obey my voice, and I will be your God, and ye shall be my people: and walk ye in all the ways that I have commanded you, that it may be well unto you. (Jer 7:23)

If the Lord imparts instruction and direction, be quick to obey. Be quick to stay in obedience to him. To be obedient to God is to stay in a teachable spirit before him.

> As an earring of gold, and an ornament of fine gold, so is a wise reprover upon an obedient ear.
> He that hath no rule over his own spirit is like a city that is broken down, and without walls. (Prov. 25:12, 28)

> And the word of God increased; and the number of the disciples multiplied in Jerusalem greatly; and a great company of the priests were obedient to the faith. (Acts 6:7)

> For to this end also did I write, that I might know the proof of you, whether ye be obedient in all things. (2 Cor 2:9)

> Let this mind be in you, which was also in Christ Jesus:
> Who, being in the form of God, thought it not robbery to be equal with God:
> But made himself of no reputation, and took upon him the form of a servant, and was made in the likeness of men:
> And being found in fashion as a man, he humbled himself, and became obedient unto death, even the death of the cross.

> Do all things without murmurings and disputings:
> That ye may be blameless and harmless, the sons of God, without rebuke, in the midst of a crooked and perverse nation, among whom ye shine as lights in the world. (Phil 2:5–8, 14–15)

Even to death on the cross did Jesus humble himself and was obedient.

Here are three more weapons:

1. Obey and be obedient.
2. Stay in a teachable spirit.
3. Do all things without complaining and disputing.

I like the story of Abigail and her foolish husband, Nabal. Nabal was a descendant of Caleb and was a wealthy sheepherder from Maon of the tribal lands of Judah. David led a band of soldiers in Judah and was often pursued by King Saul. David and his renegades protected Nabal's shepherds and protected other herds from enemy raids. At shearing time when David sent Nabal a request for food for his men, the *churlish and ill-behaved* man responded with contempt. Nabal refused to help David and his soldiers, calling David a runaway servant.

Hearing of what her foolish husband had done, Abigail intervened. Bringing provisions and soothing words to David, she stopped David from attacking and killing them. Nabal was in a drunken stupor at his house while Abigail tended to David and his soldiers. In the morning, Abigail told her husband the situation, and his "heart died within him, and he became as a stone." In ten days he died. David later claimed Abigail for his second wife.

See 1 Samuel 25 for this intriguing story.

> And when Abigail saw David, she hastened, and lighted off the ass, and fell before David on her face, and bowed herself to the ground.

And Abigail came to Nabal; and behold, he held a feast in his house, like the feast of a king; and Nabal's heart was merry with in him, for he was very drunken: wherefore she told him nothing, less or more, until the morning light.

But it came to pass in the morning, when the wine was gone out of Nabal, and his wife had told him these things, that his heart died within him, and he became as a stone.

And it came to pass about ten days after, that the Lord smote Nabal, that he died.

And Abigail hastened, and arose, and rode upon an ass, with five damsels of hers that went after her; and she went after the messengers of David, and became his wife. (1 Sam. 25:23, 36–38, 42)

Abigail humbled herself. She stayed in the right attitude, a teachable spirit, and did what she had to, to save her household from attack without complaints or disputes. Her husband had done evil for good and died.

Another story comes to mind. This one is of two kings, King Ahab of Israel and of King Jehoshaphat of Judah. Both wanted to attack the city of Ramoth-Gilead. So they gathered four hundred prophets that served the royal courts that was led by the Prophet Zedekiah.

The prophets unanimously predicted victory for the battle. However, King Jehoshaphat was suspicious of these court prophets and insisted on seeking an independent prophet. So King Ahab summoned Micaiah, warning that his prophecies were always of evils and doom to come and not favorable toward him.

Micaiah at first predicted triumph but was urged to tell the truth and recounted a vision of Israel's leaderless forces *as sheep that have no shepherd*. He also told of a vision of the Lord enthroned with the host of heaven that God sent an untruthful spirit, a lying spirit, into the mouths of the court prophets to entice King Ahab to death in battle.

The Prophet Zedekiah struck Micaiah on the cheek. King Ahab chose to believe Zedekiah's predictions of victory and put Micaiah into prison. King Ahab was killed, but King Jehoshaphat was spared and from then on stays right before God.

In 1 Samuel 22:1–35 is the recount of this story.

> Then the king of Israel gathered the prophets together, about four hundred men, and said unto them, Shall I go against Ramothgilead to battle, or shall I forbear? And they said, Go up; for the Lord shall deliver it into the hand of the king.
>
> And the king of Israel said unto Jehoshaphat, There is yet one man, Micaiah the son of Imlah, by whom we may enquire of the Lord: but I hate him; for he doth not prophesy good concerning me, but evil. And Jehoshaphat said, Let not the king say so.
>
> And he said, I saw all Israel scattered upon the hills, as sheep that have not a shepherd: and the Lord said, These have no master: let them return every man to his house in peace.
>
> And the king of Israel said unto Jehoshaphat, did I not tell thee that he would prophesy no good concerning me, but evil?
>
> And there came forth a spirit, and stood before the Lord, and said, I will pursuade him.
>
> But Zedekiah the son of Chenaanah went near, and smote Micaiah on the cheek, and said, Which way went the Spirit of the Lord from me to speak unto thee?
>
> And say, Thus saith the king, Put this fellow in the prison, and feed him with bread of afflic-

tion and with water of affliction, until I come in peace.

And the king of Israel said unto Jehoshaphat, I will disguise myself, and enter into battle; but put thou on thy robes. And the king of Israel disguised himself, and went into battle.

And the battle increased that day: and the king was stayed up in his chariot against the Syrians, and died at even: and the blood ran out of the wound into the midst of the chariot. (1 Kings 22:6, 8, 17–18, 21, 24, 27, 30, 35)

The story ends by saying Jehoshaphat did what was right in the eyes of the Lord, and he made peace with the king of Israel. He made ships to go to Ophir for gold, but they shipwrecked at Eziongeber.

Ahab's son Ahaziah took his father's place. He followed and did evil in the eyes of the Lord and served Baal and provoked the anger of God.

See 1 Kings 22:41–53 for this recount.

Two kings sought truth. Truth was delivered through a prophet. Neither king obeyed. One lived and one died. The one king that lived learned and never strayed from right before God again. The son of the other ignored the truth, served another god, did evil, and brought God's anger down on himself.

When the son wanted to join the ships, Jehoshaphat refused to have anything to do with that evil son. He had learned his lesson well.

Obedience would have saved a battle, men's lives, a king's life, and maybe the son from evil.

In both stories, we see that obedience, teachable spirit, and doing all things without complaining or disputing are weapons to be reckoned with, whether in the carnal, physical realm of battle or in the spiritual realm of battle.

> "Wherefore God also hath highly exalted him, and given him a name which is above

every name: That at the name of Jesus every knee shall bow, of things in heaven, and things in earth, and things under the earth; and that every tongue should confess that Jesus Christ is Lord, to the glory of God the Father" (Phil 2:9–11).

Jesus is over all things, and in obedience, we know he is in charge and knows what to do for us. We can fully trust him.

"Humble yourselves therefore under the mighty hand of God, that he may exalt you in due time: Casting all your care upon him; for he careth for you" (1 Peter 5:6–7).

Being obedient and casting our cares on him gives us freedom. He takes care of our troubles if we give them to him. He is God and able to handle anything you have come against you.

"Surely he hath borne our griefs, and carried our sorrows: yet we did esteem him stricken, smitten of God, and afflicted. But he was wounded for our transgressions, he was bruised for our iniquities: the chastisement of our peace was upon him; and with his strips we are healed" (Is 53:4–5).

In obedience, Jesus bore our sickness, sorrow, grief, and diseases. In obedience to him, we are free of this bondage. We can claim our healing and watch it manifest.

Jesus is our shepherd. We are the sheep. If we are in obedience in all things and are subject and submissive, we are taken care of in all things. We are to obey his directions, his commands and paths for us in all situations.

There are four weapons of victory:

1. He is Lord over all things and able to handle it.
2. He takes our cares and gives us freedom.
3. Jesus bore our ills on the cross. Claim it.
4. He is the shepherd and knows his sheep, meeting our every need.

All works for our benefits and to his glory and honor.

Chapter 7

Lots of Prayers

Prayer is a mighty weapon. In this chapter, I want to cover it rather thoroughly. I have found that when I missed God's answers to my prayers, it was me, not him, that was in error along the line. Perhaps you have experienced this also.

"*Behold*, the Lord's hand is not shortened, that it cannot save; neither his ear heavy, that it cannot hear" (Is 59:1). God both hears and reaches his hand to us. So we know that the line of communication is open.

> Beloved, if our heart condemn us not, then have we confidence toward God.
> And whatsoever we ask, we receive of him, because we keep his commandments, and do those things that are pleasing in his sight.
> And this is his commandment, That we should believe on the name of his Son Jesus Christ, and love one another, as he gave us commandment. (1 Jn 3:21–23)

We are to have confidence in God and his answers. We are to believe we receive what we ask. We are to keep his commandments and do the things that are pleasing to him. We are to believe in the name; it has power. Love one another.

> Beloved, if God so loved us, we ought also to love one another.
> No man hath seen God at any time. If we love one another, God dwelleth in us, and his love is perfected in us.
> Hereby know we that we dwell in him, and he in us, because he hath given us of his Spirit. (1 Jn 4:11–13)

> And he spake a parable unto them to this end, that men ought always to pray, and not to faint. (Luke 18:1)

This is where some wane. When we pray, we are not to faint, give up, or be discouraged if instant results are not seen. This takes practice, patience, and standing our ground. With constant faith, it will come, believing we already received it.

> From whence come wars and fightings among you? come they not hence, even of your lusts that war in your members?
> Ye lust, and have not: ye kill, and desire to have, and cannot obtain: ye fight and war, yet ye have not, because ye ask not.
> Ye ask, and receive not, because ye ask amiss, that ye may consume it upon your lusts.
> Ye adulterers and adulteresses, know ye not that the friendship of the world is enmity with God? whosoever therefore will be a friend of the world is the enemy of God. (Jas 4:1–4)

We have not because we ask not. We also ask amiss meaning. We ask generally, not specifically nor exactly. We cannot walk in the world and in God either. We have to choose one, not try to have both.

Already we see some things that need correcting right away for some.

> But if we hope for that we see not, then do we with patience wait for it.
> Likewise the Spirit also helpeth our infirmities: for we know not what we should pray for as we ought: but the Spirit itself maketh intercession for us with groanings which cannot be uttered.
> And he that searcheth the hearts knoweth what is the mind of the Spirit, because he maketh intercession for the saints according to the will of God. (Rom 8:25–27)

In the flesh, we don't know what we need to say in prayer, but the Holy Spirit in us does know. He works in the Spirit and groans in us, interceding on our behalf to the Father for us. God searches our hearts and hears the intercessions of the Spirit for us and hears the spiritual prayer. The power of the Spirit is put in motion. He also prays the will of God for our lives in every situation. He prays in groans of things we aren't even aware of.

> "And we know that all things work together for good to them that love God, to them who are called according to his purpose" (Rom 8:28).

All things, not some, work together for good for the good of us, God's children, to us that love him. This is my favorite verse in the Word. It gives me peace and settling in trials when they come. I quote this scripture *a lot*!

> "If ye abide in me, and my words abide in you, ye shall ask what ye will, and it shall be done unto you" (Jn 15:7).

If my words and I am in you, you can ask what you want, and it will be done.

Now I want to say something here. Don't be asking God ridiculous stuff. Stay in his will. Be reasonable people. If it isn't the will of God for you to win the lottery, quit asking and quit wondering why he hasn't answered your prayer!

> "And whatsoever ye shall ask in my name, that will I do, that the Father may be glorified in the Son. If ye shall ask any thing in my name, I will do it" (Jn 14:13–14).

We are to use the name of Jesus. We are to ask in the name of Jesus.

> Ye have not chosen me, but I have chosen you, and ordained you, that ye should go and bring forth fruit, and that your fruit should remain: that whatsoever ye shall ask of the Father in my name, he may give it you.
>
> These things I command you, that ye love one another.
>
> If the world hate you, ye know that it hated me before it hated you.
>
> If ye were of the world, the world would love his own: but because ye are not of the world, but I have chosen you out of the world, therefore the world hateth you. (Jn 15:16–19)

These last three verses pretty well put it in a nutshell. The world and the ruler, Satan, hates us. We were chosen, called out to live a holy life, and to do so means war. So we *have* to know what to do and how to do it.

> If any of you lack wisdom, let him ask of God, that giveth to all men liberally, and upbraideth not; and it shall be given him.
> But let him ask in faith, nothing wavering. For he that wavereth is like a wave of the sea driven with the wind and tossed.
> For let not that man think that he shall receive any thing of the Lord.
> A doubled minded man is unstable in all his ways. (Jas 1:5–8)

When we ask, we are to do so in faith and not doubt. If we doubt, we will get *nothing*! I have learned that when I need to pray, I ask how I am to pray. I don't have the knowledge and wisdom on all things, and I have to ask God on how I am to pray on things and on what I am to do and how to do them.

There are four weapons:

1. Power in the Holy Spirit
2. The Word
3. Name of Jesus
4. Faith

For prayer to be successful, we must know the Word. Ask in faith and ask in the name of Jesus. Let the Holy Spirit guide us in prayer and let him work the groaning and interceding in us.

> Seeing then that we have a great high priest, that is passed into the heavens, Jesus the Son of God, let us hold fast our profession.
> For we have not an high priest which cannot be touched with the feeling of our infirmi-

ties; but was in all points tempted like as we are, yet without sin.

Let us therefore come boldly unto the throne of grace, that we may obtain mercy, and find grace to help in time of need. (Heb 4:14–16)

Even so faith, if it hath not works, is dead, being alone. For as the body without the spirit is dead, so faith without works is dead also. (Jas 2:17, 26)

So applying your faith then is to believe you received and to confess it has already come. Hold fast to the confession.

This is where Satan swipes down now and starts doubt to go. "So you think God is going to move for you? Who are you that God will do this for you? Do you really believe he is going to bring this to pass? Do you really think he is listening to you? I don't see anything coming, and it has been three days. Come now, do you really think God isn't laughing at your asking? I don't think you understand. I'm bigger than God, and he isn't going to do anything to help you."

Does any of this sound familiar? This is where you *have* to block him out, hold fast to your confession and not go back on what you are believing for. Waver not. Be tossed not like a wave of the sea. Stand your ground.

"No, devil, he does hear me. I will have it. I do see it coming by faith. I do have it. God loves me, and he hears me. You are nothing but a legend in your own mind. God is greater than you are. You are damned now. Get behind me!"

Refuse to let doubt or fear from him enter into your heart and mind. The Word says you have what you ask, so believe the Word. It says you do and you do.

We are to pull down those imaginations and strongholds and control our minds. "(For the weapons of our warfare are not carnal, but mighty through God to the pulling down of strong holds;) Casting down imaginations, and every high thing that exalteth itself against the knowledge of God, and bringing into captivity every thought to the obedience of Christ" (2 Cor 10:4–5).

It can't get any plainer than this, saints. This is exactly what we are to do when old Satan comes calling. If he can get your faith and confession, he wins. He can get away with anything then.

Here are five steps to use against Satan and the doubt he brings:

1. Weapons are spiritual.
2. Pull down strongholds.
3. Cast down imaginations.
4. God and his knowledge is above *all*.
5. Make your thoughts to be obedient and submissive to Christ.

Dwell and meditate on what the Word says. Look up scriptures that pertain to your problem. There is an answer for anything that comes against us. Hold on to those verses, review them, think on them constantly. Look on them as if your life depends on them. Get so good at guarding your mind, heart, and confession that the devil literally shakes and trembles. Memorize the scriptures that are your answers. See yourself in your mind getting the answers and prayers coming forth. See yourself succeeding and let no failures come in to play.

> Be not ye therefore like unto them: for your Father knoweth what things ye have need of, before ye ask him.
> For if ye forgive men their trespasses, your heavenly Father will also forgive you:
> But if ye forgive not men their trespasses, neither will your Father forgive your trespasses. (Matt. 6:8, 14–15)

> But put ye on the Lord Jesus Christ, and make not provision for the flesh, to fulfil the lusts thereof. (Rom 13:14)

> My son, attend to my words; incline thine ear unto my sayings.
> Let them not depart from thine eyes; keep them in the midst of thine heart.
> For they are life unto those that find them, and health to all flesh.
> Keep thy heart with all diligence; for out of it are the issues of life. (Prov. 4:20–23)

Now God knows what we need before we even ask. But we are to pray and ask anyway. In doing so, works, faith, patience, growth, maturity, power, and strength are in us. We also need to realize that unforgiveness in us against someone will *stop* the flow of spiritual things—prayers, blessings, and success. We also are *not* forgiven either, if we don't forgive others. Again, it is *stopping* answers for our lives. There are spiritual laws that have to be followed to make things manifest on this side. There are certain things that have to be done on this side to make things on that side come to this side. We have our part that we have to do and things and laws that we have to follow to produce the end results. You can't plant green beans and expect to get watermelon; it won't work. You can't expect God to send blessings if you hate the man down the street. "But you don't know, Tania. He throws trash out his car window, and it always blows in my yard, and he does it on purpose." Maybe he does, but you can't hate him and not forgive the offense and expect God to answer a serious prayer. We have to be right before God. He searches our heart for intent and motives.

We are to make no provision for the flesh to fail. We are to prepare to succeed.

Ephesians 6:10–17 covers the armor. We have already talked in depth of this, but I want to also look at verse 18, "Praying always with all prayer and supplication in the Spirit, and watching thereunto with all perseverance and supplication for all saints."

"Prayer and supplication" are kinds of prayers. A petition is asking what we need and want, and the supplication is to claim, revere, honor, pay homage.

"In the Spirit" is to be in the Holy Spirit. Watching is to be on guard and to look, see, be alert. Perseverance is decision, persistence, keeping on, steadfast, constant for all saints. We are to be watchful and pray for each other.

I spoke of kinds of prayers. There are four kinds of prayer that changes things:

1. Petition and supplication
2. Intercession
3. Agreement
4. Binding and loosing

> Be careful for nothing; but in every thing by prayer and supplication with thanksgiving let your requests be made known unto God. (Phil 4:6)

> I *exhort* therefore, that, first of all, supplications, prayers, intercessions, and giving of thanks, be made for all men. (1 Tim. 2:1)

> Verily I say unto you, Whatsoever ye shall bind on earth shall be bound in heaven: and whatsoever shall be loose on earth shall be loosed in heaven.
> Again I say unto you, That if two of you shall agree on earth as touching any thing that they shall ask, it shall be done for them of my Father which is in heaven.
> For where two or three are gathered together in my name, there am I in the midst of them. (Matt. 18:18–20)

There is also prayer of thanksgiving and of praise covered in Philippians 4:6 and then in John 4:24, "God is a Spirit: and they that worship him must worship him in spirit and in truth." In worshipping God, we can praise and give thanks in prayer of worship.

God loves for us to minister to him.

> As they ministered to the Lord, and fasted, the Holy Ghost said, Separate me Barnabas and Saul for the work whereunto I have called them. (Acts 13:2)

> Wherefore be ye not unwise, but understanding what the will of the Lord is.
> And be not drunk with wine, wherein is excess; but be filled with the Spirit;
> Speaking to yourselves in psalms and hymns and spiritual songs, singing and making melody in your heart to the Lord;
> Giving thanks always for all things unto God and the Father in the name of our Lord Jesus Christ;
> Submitting yourselves one to another in the fear of God. (Eph 5:17–21)

And last but not least is the prayer of faith. This prayer is (1) speaking it, (2) believing it, (3) receiving it, (4) acting on it. These four things we do by faith and in faith.

> And Jesus answering saith unto them, Have faith in God.
> For verily I say unto you, That whosoever shall say unto this mountain, Be thou removed, and be thou cast into the sea; and shall not doubt in his heart, but shall believe that those things which he saith shall come to pass; he shall have whatsoever he saith.

> Therefore I say unto you, What things soever ye desire, when ye pray, believe that ye receive them, and ye shall have them.
>
> And when ye stand praying, forgive, if ye have aught against any: that your Father also which is in heaven may forgive you your trespasses.
>
> But if ye do not forgive, neither will your Father which is in heaven forgive your trespasses. (Mark 11:22–26)

Be available to God for prayer for others. Interceding on someone's behalf is a great honor. Prayer is a tool but is also communing with the Lord. Learn to develop great amounts of time in prayer with him. It will transform you. Prayer changes things as circumstances have to change. It is a mighty weapon against the enemy, Satan. There is great power in forgiveness, agreement, and harmony. Greater is he that is in us than he that is in the world. Prayer puts God and his angels on the scene. Faith gets it moving. Believing brings it in. Be a mighty prayer warrior.

Chapter 8

Secret Weapon

> If so be that ye have heard him, and have been taught by him; as the truth is in Jesus:
> That ye put off concerning the former conversation the old man, which is corrupt according to the deceitful lusts;
> And be renewed in the spirit of your mind;
> And that ye put on the new man, which after God is created in righteousness and true holiness. (Eph 4:21–24)

> And be not conformed to this world: but be ye transformed by the renewing of your mind, that ye may prove what is that good, and acceptable, and perfect, will of God.
> For I say, through the grace given unto me, to every man that is among you, not to think of himself more highly than he ought to think; but to think soberly, according as God hath dealt to every man the measure of faith. (Rom 12:2–3)

> But now ye also put off all these; anger, wrath, malice, blasphemy, filthy communication out of your mouth,
>
> Lie not one to another, seeing that ye put off the old man with his deeds;
>
> And have put on the new man, which is renewed in knowledge after the image of him that created him. (Col 3:8–10)

This chapter covers the mind—the renewed mind, the single mind, and double mind. Our mind must be the mind of Christ, or it will be unprotected for the enemy to steal. Yes, he will steal your mind if he can. Being Word minded, putting on the mind of Christ, and being obedient to renew our minds daily protects our mind. A disciplined mind, a controlled mind, is a weapon against the enemy.

The scripture says in Romans 8:31, "What shall we then say to these things? If God be for us, who can be against us?"

We have to get this down in us, people, that God himself is for us. Then who can come against us and succeed? This too is a weapon of warfare. To know and believe this verse wins in the mind before we even go into battle against the enemy. Our minds believe, have faith, and is strengthened before we even attempt to go against the foe.

> "For who hath known the mind of the Lord, that he may instruct him? But we have the mind of Christ" (1 Cor 2:16).

But we have the mind of Christ. "Do you mean I have the mind of Christ, Tania?" Yes, that is what I mean and what the scripture says. Having the mind of Christ then does what? There are four things from his mind: (1) power, (2) faith, (3) abundance, (4) healing.

Now remember what the opposites are: (1) weakness, (2) fear, (3) poverty, (4) sickness.

The world with the mind of Satan has these last four and are Satan minded, not the child of God. We have the power, faith, abundance, and healing of him.

> "But of him are ye in Christ Jesus, who of God. Is made unto us wisdom, and righteousness, and sanctification, and redemption" (1 Cor 1:30).

When the adversary strikes with distress and chaos in your life, are you going to crumble, fall into unbelief? Or are you going to stand on the promises and Word of God? Which will your mind automatically do? Reach for the Word and God or recoil in fear and be struck with confusion and terror? A renewed mind will react to the Word and God. It will be trained to reach for scriptures and promises. A daily renewed mind transforms you. You no longer operate in the human senses and carnal ways. Your mind becomes obedient to the Word and what it says. Your renewed mind transforms you into thinking as Christ does and gives you his mind.

Thoughts are the starting point of the mind, saints, the beginning of everything. Be led of the Spirit in your mind and stop relying on the old ways of the scheming of the mind.

> I *beseech* you therefore, brethren, by the mercies of God., that ye present your bodies a living sacrifice, holy, acceptable unto God, which is your reasonable service.
>
> And be not conformed to this world: but be ye transformed by the renewing of your mind, that ye may prove what is that good, and acceptable, and perfect, will of God.
>
> For I say, through the grace given unto me, to every man that is among you, not to think of himself more highly than he ought to think; but to think soberly, according as God hath dealt to every man the measure of faith. (Rom 12:1–3)

No, I am not repeating myself to hear myself but to impress you with these verses and thoughts.

Our service is to present our bodies to God as living sacrifices and be transformed by the renewing of your mind. Why? It's to prove what the good, acceptable, perfect will of God is. We are not to be legends in our own mind, and we are to think soberly with the measure of faith given you from God. Measure means proportion of faith.

> "Take therefore no thought for the morrow: for the morrow shall take thought for the things of itself. Sufficient unto the day is the evil thereof" (Matt. 6:34).

We are not to crowd our mind with all thoughts of tomorrow or of what we will eat or drink. We are to put down thoughts, control the mind with disciplined thoughts of the Word.

> "But seek ye first the kingdom of God, and his righteousness; and all these things shall be added unto you" (Matt. 6:33).

What things? These are things like what will be for dinner and what you'll wear and how will this bill get paid. Seek out God, and everything else will follow.

We are to bring into captivity every thought and cast down anything that exalts itself above God.

Read 2 Corinthians 10:3–7. We are to pull down, cast down, control, and discipline our thoughts and the mind. Why? It's because the mind is penetrated by the enemy. He will make it a battlefield of wild, wrong thoughts and will fill your mind with all kinds of junk. Becoming Christ minded protects you from that. The attacks can't get in. Have you ever heard of peace of mind? If you have crazy thoughts, attacks going on and such, you don't get peace of mind. Christ gives peace of mind and gives a sound mind.

> "But I see another law in my members, warring against the law of my mind, and bringing

me into captivity to the law of sin which is in my members" (Rom 7:23).

Thus, the battleground is in the mind. We must become single-minded in Jesus.

What is a double mind? It has one mind to please God and one mind to please self. Christians can be double minded.

"For God hath not given us the spirit of fear; but of power, and of love, and of a sound mind" (2 Tim. 1:7). Having a sound mind means to have one, not two. Single minded, one mind, the mind of Christ means to (1) serve God, (2) please God, (3) be in peace, (4) obey God, 5) rely on God.

When we fill these five steps, God will supply every need we will ever have and more.

The single mind is ruled by the Word. We receive from God, and our mind is controlled by the force of patience.

> And patience, experience; and experience, hope:
> And hope maketh not ashamed; because the love of God is shed abroad in our hearts by the Holy Ghost which is given unto us. (Rom 5:4–5)
>
> And ye shall be hated of all men for my name's sake.
> But there shall not an hair of your head perish.
> In your patience possess ye your souls. (Luke 21:17–19)

God does not allow anything to be put on us that we cannot bear or stand. We are to handle what comes our way through Christ Jesus, our strength. He will make a way of escape if need be. The trails and storms of life are what develops our patience.

We are promised a sound mind as we saw in 2 Timothy 1:7. Word-filled mind and obedient to his Word, God will supply the need that is needed. He supplies *all* our needs. God is faithful and single-minded.

> "Every good gift and every perfect gift is from above, and cometh down from the Father of lights, with whom is no variableness, neither shadow of turning" (Jas 1:17).

Single-minded is to be a doer of the Word.

> But be ye doers of the word, and not bearers only, deceiving your own selves.
> For if any be a hearer of the word, and not a doer, he is like unto a man beholding his natural face in a glass:
> For he beholdeth himself, and goeth his way, and straight way forgetteth what manner of man he was.
> But whoso looketh into the perfect law of liberty, and continueth therein, he being not a forgetful hearer, but a doer of the work, this man shall be blessed in his deed. (Jas 1:22–25)

Single-minded is sober and sound in patience and faith. "That the aged men be sober, grave, temperate, sound in faith, in charity, in patience" (Titus 2:2).

When you have a chance, read all of chapter 2 of Titus. It gives a clear picture of this verse.

Have you ever heard of the mind being connected to your tongue? Confessing the Word controls our mind and keeps our thinking straight.

> Casting down imaginations, and every high thing that exalteth itself against the knowledge of God, and bringing into captivity every thought to the obedience of Christ;

And having in a readiness to revenge all disobedience, when your obedience is fulfilled. (2 Cor 10:5–6)

And the peace of God, which passeth all understanding, shall keep your hearts and minds through Christ Jesus. (Phil 4:7)

A great weapon for the mind against the enemy is Philippians 4:8, "Finally, brethren, whatsoever things are true, whatsoever things are honest, whatsoever things are lovely, whatsoever things are of good report; if there be any praise, think on these things."

Derek is Hebrew for conversation. The Bible refers to many different meanings on this word.

1. To tread

    "Wherefore art thou red in thine apparel, and thy garments like him that treadeth in the winefat?" (Is 63:2).

2. To bend

    "And they bend their tongues like their bow for lies: but they are not valiant for the truth upon the earth; for they proceed from evil to evil, and they know not me, saith the Lord" (Jer 9:3).

3. Sweet converse

    "And this man shall be the peace, when the Assyrian shall come into our land; and when he shall tread in our palaces, then shall we raise against him seven shepherds, and eight principal men" (Mic. 5:5).

The mind once made up then has the heart to complement and confirm the mind's action or decision:

1. Understanding

    "But I have understanding as well as you; I am not inferior to you: yea, who knoweth not such things as these?" (Job 12:3).

2. Will, purpose

    "And his armourbearer said unto him, Do all that is in thine heart: turn thee; behold, I am with thee according to thy heart" (1 Sam. 14:7).

3. Thinking and acting

    "Create in me a clean heart, O God; and renew a right spirit within me. Cast me not away from thy presence; and take not thy holy spirit from me. Restore unto me the joy of thy salvation; and uphold me with thy free spirit" (Ps 51:10–12).

The word *mind* at times can be translated as heart. "My soul longeth, yea, even fainteth for the courts of the Lord: my heart and my flesh crieth out for the living God" (Ps 84:2).

"Yeah, but, Tania, I have a guy I know that causes me problems every which way he can. I practice what the Word says and try to renew my mind but—"

The following weapons are to be used here. "Therefore if thine enemy hunger, feed him; if he thirst, give him drink: for in so doing thou shalt heap coals of fire on his head. Be not overcome of evil, but overcome evil with good" (Rom 12:20–21).

When you feed and give a cup of water to your enemy, give back good when they do bad and evil to you. You snare the roaring lion, the devil in his own trap. You turn the fiery darts around from you and are aiming them back at him. You are overcoming the enemy. Satan will use who he can against you. So the next time the neighbor man lets his dog think your yard is his private toilet, go out and be friendly to the man. He will move on or get some manners quickly.

Many are our weapons against Satan. We just need to know what some are and that it is okay to use them. Be a doer of the Word. Be a mover and a shaker. Your heart will be persuaded.

Chapter 9

What Satan Saw

I want to share something with you. I was reading one day about the day of Pentecost. It suddenly struck me what all Satan had seen that day. The Lord showed me all at once it seemed.

Satan saw

1. the Holy Ghost—the power of what cast him out of heaven enter into those men and women.
2. New birth—he saw them recreated and as new creatures having their sins blotted out.
3. Immortality—he watched eternal life enter into them.
4. Jesus's name—given that day for them to use with all authority, to do miracles, and to be who they were in Christ.
5. Liberty—his hold on them and he saw a new awakening of freedom from him.

I was reading along, and all of a sudden this all hit me. I guess I had already known it in the back of my mind but never had really looked at it quite this way before. I had only focused on the part where the Comforter, the Holy Spirit, had come as Jesus had promised and that he had conquered the devil and taken away the authority from him but had not looked at it through Satan's eyes until God revealed it to me as I was reading.

And just what does all this have to do with war and weapons? It gives us five inherited treasures that Jesus gave us when he laid his life down:

1. Salvation (Heb 1:14)
2. His name (Acts 4:12, Matt. 10:6–8)
3. The earth (Eph 4:13)
4. The heavenly kingdom (Col 2:3)
5. Abraham's promise (Gal 3:29)

This means the righteousness of God is now ours. The struggle is over.

> Are they not all ministering spirits, sent forth to minister for them who shall be heirs of salvation? (Heb 1:14)

> Neither is there salvation in any other: for there is none other name under heaven given among men, whereby we must be saved. (Acts 4:12)

> But go rather to the lost sheep of the house of Israel:
> And as ye go, preach, saying, The kingdom of heaven is at hand.
> Heal the sick, cleanse the lepers, raise the dead, cast out devils: freely ye have received, freely give. (Matt. 10:6–8)

> Till we all come in the unity of the faith, and of the knowledge of the Son of God, unto a perfect man, unto the measure of the stature of the fulness of Christ. (Eph 4:13)

> In whom are hid all the treasures of wisdom and knowledge. (Col 2:3)

> And if ye be Christ's, then are ye Abraham's seed, and heirs according to the promise. (Gal 3:29)

Being children of God gives us all the same standing with him because righteousness can't be obtained through works we may do. It is a gift from the Father.

> What shall we say then? That the Gentiles, which followed not after righteousness, have attained to righteousness, even the righteousness which is of faith.
> But Israel, which followed after the law of righteousness, hath not attained to the law of righteousness.
> Wherefore? Because they sought it not by faith, but as it were by the works of the law. For they stumbled at that stumblingstone. (Rom 9:30–32)

God's righteousness stops sin. "Awake to righteousness, and sin not; for some have not the knowledge of God: I speak this to your shame" (1 Cor 15:34).

God sees us in righteousness right standing before him. Through his eyes, we are not in sin any longer when we are his.

> Who being the brightness of his glory, and the express image of his person, and upholding all things by the word of his power, when he had by himself purged our sins, sat down on the right hand of the Majesty on high. (Heb 1:3)

> Which was a figure for the time then present, in which were offered both gifts and sacrifices, that could not make him that did the service perfect, as pertaining to the conscience;
>
> How much more shall the blood of Christ, who through the eternal Spirit offered himself without spot to God, purge your conscience from the dead works to serve the living God? (Heb 9:9, 14)
>
> For then would they not have ceased to be offered? because that the worshippers once purged should have had no more conscience of sins. (Heb 10:2)

To recreate himself in us is the purpose of God. We accept Jesus sacrifice, and God accepts us as though sin had never been in us. God's righteousness is a gift to us.

> "For if by one man's offence death reigned by one; much more they which receive abundance of grace and of the gift of righteousness shall reign in life by one, Jesus Christ" (Rom 5:17).

So we must learn to depend on this gift—righteousness.

> "Ye are of God, little children, and have overcome them: because greater is he that is in you, than he that is in the world" (1 Jn 4:4).

Further down, look at verse 6, "We are of God: he that knoweth God heareth us; he that is not of God heareth not us. Hereby know we the spirit of truth, and the spirit of error."

The spirit of truth and the spirit of error—we know these both being of God. "Okay, Tania, so what does knowing these two spirits do for me?"

Well, in righteousness the struggle for us is over, and we walk in victory. We grow up in him in all things. We produce peace and quiet.

> But speaking the truth in love, may grow up into him in all things, which is the head, even Christ. (Eph 4:15)

> And the work of righteousness shall be peace; and the effect of righteousness quietness and assurance forever.
> And my people shall dwell in a peaceable habitation, and in sure dwellings, and in quiet resting places. (Is 32:17–18)

In his righteousness we are able to stand before our Father without guilt or condemnation. We have our needs met, protection and security, peace and quiet. The victory is in Jesus. We mature in all things. We develop righteous consciousness. God is recreated in us as we grow and move into the things of him. Unity of all things is his plan, speaking truth in love and us all being as one. Knowing our rights in Jesus, our standing in him, we rise up in him.

We have access to all that is the Father's. "Therefore let no man glory in men. For all things are yours; Whether Paul, or Apollos, or Cephas, or the world, or life, or death, or things present, or things to come; all are yours; And ye are Christ's; and Christ is God's" (1 Cor 3:21–23).

To me, to be a righteous warrior of God is to be possessed with integrity. My self, thoughts, and words with actions are to so shine that God is glorified in all I do to take all that I know and defeat the enemy until I go home.

Who can count the dust of Jacob, and the number of the fourth part of Israel? Let me die the death of the righteous, and let my last end be like his! (Num. 23:10)

Drop down, ye heavens, from above, and let the skies pour down righteousness: let the earth open, and let them bring forth salvation, and let righteousness spring up together; I the Lora nave created it. (Is 45:8)

God is saying here, "Let prosperity rain down on the just and righteous." The following scriptures pertain to weapons of war through righteousness. Drink them into your being.

Arise, o Lord; save me, O my God: for thou hast smitten all mine enemies upon the cheek bone; thou hast broken the teeth of the ungodly.
Salvation belongeth unto the Lord: thy blessing is upon thy people. Se'lah. (Ps 3:7–8)

But let all those that put their trust in thee rejoice: let them ever shout for joy, because thou defendest them: let them also that love thy name be joyful in thee.
For thou, Lord, wilt bless the righteous; with favor wilt thou compass him as with a shield. (Ps 5:11–12)

He restoreth my soul: he leadeth me in the paths of righteousness for his names' sake.
Yea, though I walk through the valley of the shadow of death, I will fear no evil: for thou art with me; thy rod and thy staff they comfort me.

Thou preparest a table before me in the presence of mine enemies: thou anointest my head with oil; my cup runneth over.

Surely goodness and mercy shall follow me all the days of my life: and I will dwell in the house of the Lord for ever. (Ps 23:3–6)

O taste and see that the Lord is good: blessed is the man that trusteth in him.

O fear the Lord, ye his saints: for there is no want to them that fear him.

The young lions do lack, and suffer hunger: but they that seek the Lord shall not want any good thing.

Come, ye children, hearken unto me: I will teach you the fear of the Lord. (Ps 34:8–11)

For a day in thy courts is better than a thousand. I had rather be a doorkeeper in the house of my God, than to dwell in the tents of wickedness.

For the Lord God is a sun and shield: the Lord will give grace and glory: no good thing will he withhold from them that walk uprightly.

O Lord of hosts, blessed is the man that trusteth in thee. (Ps 84:10–12)

Truth shall spring out of the earth; and righteousness shall look down from heaven.

Yea, the Lord shall give that which is good; and our land shall yield her increase.

Righteousness shall go before him; and shall set us in the way of his steps. (Ps 85:11–13)

The fear of the wicked, it shall come upon him: but the desire of the righteous shall be granted.

> As the whirlwind passeth, so is the wicked no more: but the righteous is an everlasting foundation. (Prov. 10:24–25)

> The righteousness of the perfect shall direct his way: but the wicked shall fall by his own wickedness.
> The righteousness of the upright shall deliver them: but transgressors shall be taken in their own naughtiness. (Prov. 11:5–6)

> A man shall not be established by wickedness: but the root of the righteous shall not be moved. (Prov. 12:3)

> The wicked are overthrown, and are not: but the house of the righteous shall stand. (Prov. 12:7)

The Word is full of such scriptures as I have shared of the righteousness and victory. As you have seen, righteousness of God in us is a mighty weapon against the devil, Lucifer. It breaks the bonds of Satan against us and frees us to be who we are in Jesus and his righteousness.

> In the way of righteousness is life; and in the pathway thereof there is no death. (Prov. 12:28)

> And I saw heaven opened, and behold a white horse; and he that sat upon him was called Faithful and True, and in righteousness he doth Judge and make war.
> His eyes were as a flame of fire, and on his head were many crowns; and he had a name written, that no man knew, but he himself.

> And he was clothed with a vesture dipped in blood: and his name is called The Word of God. (Rev. 19:11–13)

This is where he will lead the saints to earth and the great battle with Satan comes, the battle of all battles, when the Lord takes back the earth from Satan and reclaims the stolen property once and for all. We live now to regain and claim while we are in the earth to practice, if you will, how to handle and rule. We are of a royal priesthood. Jesus reclaimed it all on the cross, gave it us to take care of until his return. Stop letting the devil be in charge. Take your place as the bought overcomer that you are. In God's army, there are no wimps or cowards.

> "But ye are a chosen generation, a royal priesthood, an holy nation, a peculiar people; that ye should shew forth the praises of him who hath called you out of darkness into his marvellous light: Which in time past were not a people, but are now the people of God: which had not obtained mercy, but now have obtained mercy" (1 Peter 2:9–10).

If we all walked in the light, we had put into action all we knew. The devil would be in constant terror and would not be running rampant in the lives of the saved, let alone the earth, and Christ would return sooner. My favorite verse on the devil is this one in Isaiah 14:15–16, "Yet thou shalt be brought down to hell, to the sides of the pit. They that see thee shall narrowly look upon thee, and consider thee, saying, Is this the man that made the earth to tremble, that did shake kingdoms."

Chapter 10

Power in Praise

There are so many topics I could choose to cover in this last chapter, things like fasting, love, our emotions, and the list goes on. All are weapons, but I choose to cover the committed life and the power of praise.

Many people are saved, but when the going gets rough, they backslide and bail out on God. Thus, the committed life is laying down your life. I'm talking about taking your life and offering it up completely. No holds barred is a committed life. How can this be a weapon you ask? When you do this, you're giving it *all* to God the Father. You're saying in essence, "Here, Lord, I'm completely yours. Though you slay me, still will I trust you." You're settled, sold out, and totally his. No looking back, no regrets. You are fully persuaded, heart, soul, and mind. Your heels are dug in. You are committed until it hurts if need be.

> "And being fully persuaded that, what he had promised, he was able also to perform" (Rom 4:21).

God promised Abraham and Sarah a child. Abraham was fully persuaded that God was able and would do it.

No matter what, you have to be persuaded also. No matter how things look or what people say or how it is going, you are committed that God is able.

"And hereby we know that we are of the truth, and shall assure our hearts before him" (1 Jn 3:19). Here we know we are of the truth, meaning of God, and we shall persuade or assure our hearts before him of it. This chapter of John talks of love and loving your brother as Christ loves us and that we should lay down our life for the brethren. See verse 16.

Then this committed life leads to settling down in your heart and soul who you are, what you're doing, your purpose or call, and that God is in control. You will follow what the Word says to do. You will listen to God and learn his ways. Be a man or woman of God. Go deeper into the things of God. God is only limited because *you* limit him. Some people are happy with just salvation while others wade out deeper, wanting more and more of him, wanting that relationship like Enoch, Moses, Abraham, and David had with him, wanting only the best for themselves which is only from the Father. Settling who is first place, settling who meets your needs, settling who guides you—that is Jesus. This closes the door to you. The enemy can't get at you as easily. He can't get your eyes off Jesus. He can't confuse you about who your source and master is. He can't play with your heart and put doubt in your mind when you know that you know Jesus is Lord over your life, and you're sold out.

If you try to be in the world and be a Christian, the devil will play havoc with you. Many of you are experiencing this. Choose today who is your master. Get off the fence and choose God. Be on the winning side. Watch your life become steady and sure as he guides you.

> But the hour cometh, and now is, when the true worshippers shall worship the Father in spirit and in truth: for the Father seeketh such to worship him.

> God is a Spirit: and they that worship him must worship him in spirit and in truth. (Jn 4:23–24)

> Let the word of Christ dwell in you richly in all wisdom; teaching and admonishing one another in psalms and hymns and spiritual songs, singing with grace in your hearts to the Lord.
> And whatsoever ye do in word or deed, do all in the name of the Lord Jesus, giving thanks to God and the Father by him. (Col 3:16–17)

There is mighty power in worship and praise. It brings God on the scene. It breaks you free from the enemy. It works confidence in you for God to deliver you or see you through the storm. It builds your spirit up, strengthening you. It keeps your eyes on Jesus and his Word and instruction. It brings you closer to him. It moves mountains. It brings the ministering angels to your side. When was the last time you went before the throne to just be in his presence to tell him you love him and to thank him for all he has done and is doing?

> "I have seen his ways, and will heal him: I will lead him also, and restore comforts unto him and to his mourners. I create the fruit of the lips; Peace, peace to him that is far off, and to him that is near, saith the Lord; and I will heal him" (Is 57:18–19).

Praise and worship brings peace and fruits of our lips. The wicked have no peace in verse 21 as the Word says. So are we to praise and worship only when we are in a storm from the devil? No, we are to praise and worship continually as the Word says.

> "By him therefore let us offer the sacrifice of praise to God continually, that is, the fruit of our lips giving thanks to his name. But to do good

and to communicate forget not: for with such sacrifices God is well pleased" (Heb 13:15–16).

Not only do we continually praise and worship, but God sees this as sacrifices to him: (1) praise, 2) worship, (3) sacrifices.

> "Out of the mouth of babes and sucklings hast thou ordained strength because of thine enemies, that thou mightest still the enemy and the avenger" (Ps 8:2).

Praise and worship gives strength and stills the enemy, the devil.

"Yeah, but, Tania, it is just too hard to praise God when you're in a crisis." It seems silly to do this when you're being bombarded by the enemy. That's a weapon the enemy uses on you. Reverse it. Praise God for what he has done, is doing, and is going to do. Watch it all turn around. Watch what the power of praise does for you, around you, and in you.

"But thou art holy, O thou that inhabitest the praises of Israel" (Ps 22:3). God inhabits our praises and worship. The presence of God turns back the enemy.

> When mine enemies are turned back, they shall fall and perish at thy presence.
> The Lord also will be a refuge for the oppressed, a refuge in times of trouble. (Ps 9:3, 9)

> The Lord preserveth all them that love him: but all the wicked will he destroy. (Ps 145:20)

> Because he hath set his love upon me, therefore will I deliver him: I will set him on high, because he hath known my name. (Ps 91:14)

> And he said unto them, Verily I say unto you, There is no man that hath left house, or

parents, or brethren, or wife, or children, for the kingdom of God's sake,
Who shall not receive manifold more in this present time, and in the world to come life everlasting. (Luke 18:29–30)

When I think of a committed life, Paul comes to mind. Through the many years of travel, churches were born. Lives were changed. Through trials and storms, Paul was undaunted, committed to his call, committed to Christ. He wrote to Timothy, "I am already on the point of being sacrificed. The time of my departure has come. I have fought the good fight. I have finished the race. I have kept the faith." See 2 Timothy 4:6–7. Throughout the history of Christianity, Paul's powerful formulation of the gospel and his emphasis on salvation by the grace of God through faith in Jesus and his focus on love as the central value of Christian life has served as a beacon for the church's greatest theologians. Paul, a man with insight and spirit, a truly committed apostle and soldier, was a man of faith. Paul was beheaded in Rome according to tradition.

The Lord shall cause thine enemies that rise up against thee to be smitten before thy face: they shall come out against thee one way, and flee before thee seven ways. (Deut. 28:7)

For the Lord your God is he that goeth with you, to fight for you against your enemies, to save you. (Deut. 26:4)

Through God we shall do valiantly: for he it is that shall tread down our enemies. (Ps 60:12)

When a man's ways please the Lord, he maketh even his enemies to be at peace with him. (Ps 16:7)

So that we may boldly say, The Lord is my helper, and I will not fear what man shall do unto me. (Heb 13:6)

Not by might nor by power but, by my Spirit says the Lord Almighty. (Zech. 4:6)

Put on the whole armour of God, that ye may be able to stand against the wiles of the devil.

For we wrestle not against flesh and blood, but against principalities, against powers, against the rulers of the darkness of this world, against spiritual wickedness in high places.

Wherefore take unto you the whole armour of God, that ye may be able to withstand in the evil day, and having done all, to stand.

Stand therefore, having your loins girt about with truth, and having on the breastplate of righteousness;

And your feet shod with the preparation of the gospel of peace;

Above all, taking the shield of faith, wherewith ye shall be able to quench all the fiery darts of the wicked.

And take the helmet of salvation, and the sword of the spirit, which is the word of God:

Praying always with all prayer and supplication in the Spirit, and watching thereunto with all perseverance and supplication for all the saints. (Eph 6:11–18)

Chapter 11

Receive Him

"That if thou shalt confess with thy mouth the Lord Jesus, and shalt believe in thine heart that God hath raised him from the dead, thou shalt be saved. For with the heart man believeth unto righteousness; and with the mouth confession is made unto salvation" (Romans 10:9–10).

To receive Jesus into your heart, simply pray this prayer from your heart, "Jesus, I believe you died for me and you rose on the third day. I confess I am a sinner and ask you for forgiveness. Come into my heart and life now and be Lord over me. I confess you now as my Savior and Lord. Amen."

Let me be the first to welcome you into the family of God, and may his love abound toward you.

ABOUT THE AUTHOR

Tania was born and raised in Seymour, Indiana. She was a graduate of Seymour High School, graduate of missionary ministries from the Kings Cross Victory Bible College with doctorate degree, ordained licensed by First Church of the Gospel Ministry, ordained licensed by Universal Ministries. She was also a graduate of Berean Bible College and American Association of Christian Counselors Institute for biblical counseling and discipleship with courses online. She volunteered as an assistant chaplain for Southern Indiana Hospice, volunteered for chaplain at Seymour Schneck Hospital. She was the founder of Faith in Flight jail ministry and bible ministry and was the guest speaker and teacher. She was an evangelist and author of various published poems and Christian articles in various magazines. She was married with three children and two grandchildren. She's nondenominational and would work with all ministries.